THE SECRET OF THE SAINTS

Chris John-Terry

THE SECRET OF THE SAINTS

"Strive after the greater gifts.
And I point out to you a yet more excellent way."
— Saint Paul, 1 Cor 12:31

ALBA·HOUSE   NEW·YORK

SOCIETY OF ST. PAUL, 2187 VICTORY BLVD., STATEN ISLAND, NEW YORK 10314

ST PAULS

Library of Congress Cataloging-in-Publication Data

John-Terry, Chris.
    The secret of the saints / Chris-John Terry.
        p. cm.
    Includes bibliographical references.
    ISBN 0-8189-0864-5
    1. Spirituality — Catholic Church. 2. Mysticism — Catholic
Church. I. Title.
BX2350.65.J63   1999
248 — dc21   99-20572
                                        CIP

Produced and designed in the United States of America by the
Fathers and Brothers of the Society of St. Paul,
2187 Victory Boulevard, Staten Island, New York 10314-6603,
as part of their communications apostolate.

ISBN: 0-8189-0864-5

Printing Information:

Current Printing - first digit 1 2 3 4 5 6 7 8 9 10

Year of Current Printing - first year shown

1999   2000   2001   2002   2003   2004   2005   2006

TABLE OF CONTENTS

INTRODUCTION

Anybody who talks about mysticism today is likely to receive some adverse criticism. He might be accused of being presumptuous in speaking of a mysterious knowledge or experience that is, properly speaking, the possession only of the saints. Or he might be suspected of teaching occult doctrines that have no place in a scientifically enlightened world. Likewise, anybody who often goes to church, or who performs pious exercises leading to a deeper interior life, is likely to suffer similar misunderstanding. His acquaintances might accuse him of fanaticism and his inclination toward solitude and recollection might result in his being isolated from their company.

One reason why many people have a feeling of antipathy toward those who live a profound interior life is a certain *ignorance* or *prejudice* concerning the nature of sanctity. Some have identified it with the extraordinary supernatural phenomena that God sometimes grants to the saints, such as private revelations, the stigmata, levitation, the luminous and fragrant effluvia, and the like. These phenomena are strictly gratuitous gifts, and a person cannot ordinarily acquire them by his personal efforts alone. So, when people hear that somebody is working to be a saint or a mystic, they think that this person is merely wishing to receive these extraordinary gifts himself. They laugh at him, thinking that he is vain.

Another reason for the ill feeling that some have towards the devout life is *skepticism*. This is especially true of the learned and the clever, those who are full of worldly wisdom, but who lack the spirituality to recognize the work of God in favored souls. These people are quick to dismiss mystical experiences as foolish simply because they, who spent very little time in prayer, have not had these experiences themselves. Saint John of the Cross rightly compares them to the scribes and the Pharisees. Our Lord censured them because they themselves had not entered into that kind of life, and those who were coming in they hindered. "Woe to you scribes and Pharisees, hypocrites: because you shut the kingdom of heaven against men, for you yourselves do not enter in; and those that are going in, you suffer not to enter" (Mt 23:13).

This book aims to remove some of the prejudices and misconceptions that many have about the spiritual life. Some people do not advance on the road to holiness because they think that sanctity is not for them. "I shall never become a saint," they say. "It is enough for me to be saved." But this excuse contains a basic fallacy. Sanctity is necessary because in heaven there will only be saints.

Of course, sanctity is a *free gift*. But for that matter, even salvation itself is a free gift (Eph 2:1-10), and one cannot hope to be saved without *willing* to be a saint!

I am aware that many religious writers have already written excellent treatises on this subject. The works of Saint John of the Cross and Saint Teresa of Avila are still in print. The theological writings of more recent authors, such as Father Reginald Garrigou-Lagrange, John Arintero and Jordan Aumann, are also readily available. However, their books are as long as they are thorough. In the present world very few people have the time and the endurance to read voluminous masterpieces of spiritual literature. I thought that it is good to have a much shorter book that will also give the substance and precision of these longer works, and which would be less intimidating. This is why I wrote this book. I did not write it for the skeptical. Words do not have the same meaning for them as for those who believe. This book is for those who have faith, but who want depth and direction in their spiritual lives.

Biblical Abbreviations

OLD TESTAMENT

Genesis	Gn	Nehemiah	Ne	Baruch	Ba
Exodus	Ex	Tobit	Tb	Ezekiel	Ezk
Leviticus	Lv	Judith	Jdt	Daniel	Dn
Numbers	Nb	Esther	Est	Hosea	Ho
Deuteronomy	Dt	1 Maccabees	1 M	Joel	Jl
Joshua	Jos	2 Maccabees	2 M	Amos	Am
Judges	Jg	Job	Jb	Obadiah	Ob
Ruth	Rt	Psalms	Ps	Jonah	Jon
1 Samuel	1 S	Proverbs	Pr	Micah	Mi
2 Samuel	2 S	Ecclesiastes	Ec	Nahum	Na
1 Kings	1 K	Song of Songs	Sg	Habakkuk	Hab
2 Kings	2 K	Wisdom	Ws	Zephaniah	Zp
1 Chronicles	1 Ch	Sirach	Si	Haggai	Hg
2 Chronicles	2 Ch	Isaiah	Is	Malachi	Ml
Ezra	Ezr	Jeremiah	Jr	Zechariah	Zc
		Lamentations	Lm		

NEW TESTAMENT

Matthew	Mt	Ephesians	Eph	Hebrews	Heb
Mark	Mk	Philippians	Ph	James	Jm
Luke	Lk	Colossians	Col	1 Peter	1 P
John	Jn	1 Thessalonians	1 Th	2 Peter	2 P
Acts	Ac	2 Thessalonians	2 Th	1 John	1 Jn
Romans	Rm	1 Timothy	1 Tm	2 John	2 Jn
1 Corinthians	1 Cor	2 Timothy	2 Tm	3 John	3 Jn
2 Corinthians	2 Cor	Titus	Tt	Jude	Jude
Galatians	Gal	Philemon	Phm	Revelation	Rv

THE SECRET OF THE SAINTS

CHAPTER 1

LIVING THE LIFE OF GOD

The Essence of Sanctity

A large amount of prejudice concerning the heroic life of the saints may be removed by having a proper understanding of the nature of *grace*. Many people equate sanctity with the ability to perform miracles and other marvelous deeds. They regard a person very highly if he can cast out demons, heal the sick, read minds, or perform other spectacular feats. In truth, however, sanctity does not consist in any of these. A saint is not necessarily a "wonder-worker." True, we have heard of saints, such as Saint Martin de Porres, who talked to animals. Others, such as Saint Anthony of Padua, were said to have been seen in two places at the same time. However, such accomplishments are entirely charismatic. They are beyond the power of any human creature to accomplish. God Himself is the one who performs these wonders through them.

These extraordinary gifts, such as being in two places at the same time, casting out demons, prophesying future events, *etc.,* are accidental to sanctity as such. God freely grants them to some people, not necessarily to show the sanctity of the recipients, but to edify the faithful. In the Gospel of Saint Matthew we read our Lord Jesus saying, "Many will say to me on that day: Lord, Lord, did we not prophesy in your name, and drive out demons in your name, and do mighty works in your name? And then will I declare to them, I never knew you: depart from me, you pack of evildoers" (Mt 7:22-23). Christ's words imply that even wicked people sometimes receive the gift to prophesy or the power to cast out demons, but that does not necessarily make them pleasing to God. Therefore, there is something more essential to sanctity than the power to perform miracles, and that is, the living of the divine life through *grace*.

What exactly is sanctifying grace? The *Catechism of the Catholic Church* defines it as an habitual gift, a stable and supernatural disposition that perfects the soul itself to enable it to live with God and to act by his love. It is the free and undeserved help that God gives us to respond to his call to become children of God, adoptive sons and daughters, partakers of the divine nature and of eternal life. In other words, it is a participation in the life of God himself.

According to this understanding, grace is not something that merely gives us a right to eternal life. Rather, it is something that *changes* and *elevates* our nature without destroying it.[1] Sanctifying grace

---

[1] Saint Thomas Aquinas, *Summa Theologiae,* Part I, q. 1, art. 8, Reply to Obj. 2. Tr. by The Fathers of the English Dominican Province in *Summa Theologica* (Benziger Brothers, Inc. 1947).

is something that enables us to live not merely our natural life, but the life of God Himself.

We do not know intimately what grace is because we do not have a direct knowledge of God's Essence and Life, of which grace is a participation. All that we know is that grace is the beginning of eternal life in us, the seed of the Divine Life in our soul. Since this life of grace belongs to the supernatural order, it is preeminently higher than every form of natural life, whether of men or of angels. So Saint Thomas Aquinas does not hesitate to say, "The good of grace in one (person) is greater than the good of nature in the whole universe."[2]

If we are in the state of grace, we possesses the life of God in our souls. The Holy Spirit vivifies us and enables us to live as children of God. This union of the human life and the Divine Life is at first imperceptible. But as we become more faithful to the promptings of the Holy Spirit, we also become increasingly aware of the divine life within. Eventually, such awareness reaches the realm of consciousness and we become *mystics*. Through the gifts of the Holy Spirit, particularly the gift of wisdom, we acquire a kind of divine sense or instinct by which we perceive God Himself. Although in this life we do not see God face to face, we can

---

[2] Saint Thomas Aquinas, *Summa Theologiae*, Part I-II, q. 113, art. 9, Reply to Obj. 2.

perceive what God wills, converse with Him, and enjoy the familiarity of the Divine Persons.

Therefore, it is important to recognize the value of sanctifying grace in our spiritual life. Sanctifying grace does more than merely wash away our sins, as we learn in the catechism. It also enlarges our nature and opens it to the influx of Divine Life. What we call the "mystical life" is actually the flowering, or the summit, of the life of grace in our soul. In this sense it is not something extraordinary, for it is the normal result of a life lived in full conformity with God's Will. Mysticism may not be a common phenomenon, for sanctity in the world is not common. But mysticism as a lived experience is not uncommon among those who live a profoundly spiritual life.

People often say that miracles are the shadow of sanctity because they usually go with saintly persons. However, it is the life of grace itself and not the miracles that essentially constitutes sanctity. As a man is more important than his shadow, so grace is more important than miracles and extraordinary gifts. Saint Thomas says that sanctifying grace is nobler than the extraordinary gifts such as prophecy, miracles, *etc.*[3] For sanctifying grace makes us participators in God's own life, whereas the extraordinary gifts only serve to edify the faithful or to

[3] Saint Thomas, *Summa Theologiae,* Part I-II, q. 111, art. 5

confirm divine teaching. The life of grace is nothing else than a prelude to that eternal life that the Blessed in heaven enjoy.

In heaven our happiness will consist in beholding the Divine Essence, or in seeing God "face to face." In heaven the Blessed see God, not through the things that He has made (as the philosophers do), nor in the darkness of a living faith (as the mystics on earth do), but as He Himself is. "We know," Saint John says, "that when he shall appear, we shall be like him: because we shall see him as he is" (1 Jn 3:2). This immediate vision of God, which one normally attains only in the next life, surpasses the natural capacity of every created intellect. To behold God face to face, therefore, it is necessary that we receive a higher light than the natural light of our intellect. In heaven God gives us this superior light — what theologians call the "light of glory" (*lumen gloriae*). This light increases the capacity of our intellect, and enables it to see the Divine Essence in its sovereign simplicity and beauty.[4]

---

[4] A person who is still on earth cannot *naturally* see God in His Essence, but only through certain images or concepts (*ST* I, q. 12, art. 11). However, it is possible for a person (*e.g.,* St. Paul), while still on earth, to have an intellectual vision of God in His Essence if, by a *miraculous intervention,* God increases the natural light of the intellect (*ST* I, q. 12, art. 11, Reply to Obj. 2). This added light is similar to the light of glory that is given to the saints in heaven, except that it is granted not perpetually but only transiently (*ST* II-II, q. 175, art. 3, Reply to Obj. 2).

Is Friendship with God Possible?

In his famous book, *The Three Ages of the Interior Life,* Fr. Reginald Garrigou-Lagrange notes that in Antiquity the barbarians thought that perfection consisted mainly in *fortitude;* the Greek philosophers thought that it consisted chiefly in *wisdom;* but the Gospels teach that it consists principally in acts of *charity.*[5] A life of charity and Christian perfection is essentially a life of grace. This life of grace increases in proportion as a person becomes more completely united to God through charity.

Charity is not mere love of God. Even a sinful man can love God, that is, simply as a desirable object. Charity is more than the love of a desirable object. It implies reciprocity and friendship. Charity is the mutual love between God and man. It is a love of friendship that makes one heart of two. For charity to exist, therefore, it is not enough that we love God. It is also necessary that God love us. And we know that He does. In fact, "We love God because He first loved us" (1 Jn 4:19). This is why charity is something supernatural. It requires God's love or *friendship.* This is also why charity

---

[5] Cf. Reginald Garrigou-Lagrange, OP, *The Three Ages of the Interior Life,* tr. by Sister M. Timothea Doyle, OP (Rockford, IL: TAN Books and Publishers, Inc., 1989), Vol. 1, Ch. 8, p. 145.

presupposes grace, for it is grace alone that adequately disposes the human person for a love of friendship with God.

Is friendship with God possible? The Greek philosopher, Aristotle, does not think so. For him, there cannot be friendship between man and God because friendship requires a certain degree of equality between the lover and the beloved. But between man and God there is a great inequality. "How could any kind of friendship exist between Jupiter and man?" Aristotle asks. For Aristotle, friendship with God is impossible.[6]

For his part, Saint Thomas Aquinas asserts that friendship with God *is* possible, but this fact is not discovered by reason. Rather, it is a revealed truth, an article of faith.[7] It is as much an object of faith as grace itself is, for it is grace that makes friendship with God possible. By raising a person to the supernatural order, grace makes him partake of the very life and goods of God Himself. In this manner a person attains that kind of "equality" that meets the fundamental requirement for true friendship.

So, charity presupposes grace, although it is charity that formally unites a person to God. For

---

[6] Aristotle, *Nicomachean Ethics,* Book VIII, Ch. 7.

[7] It is revealed in John 15:15: "I no longer call you servants... But I have called you friends... "

this reason, charity is above all other virtues, above fortitude, above wisdom. Saint Paul teaches that charity is superior even to miracles and other extraordinary gifts:

> Strive after the greater gifts. And I point out to you a yet more excellent way. If I should speak with the tongues of men and of angels, but do not have charity, I have become as sounding brass or tinkling cymbal. And if I have prophecy and know all mysteries and all knowledge, and if I have all faith so as to remove mountains, yet do not have charity, I am nothing. And if I distribute all my goods to feed the poor, and if I deliver my body to be burned, yet do not have charity, it profits me nothing (1 Cor 12:31; 13:1-3).

Jesus and Mary

No one becomes a friend of God except through Christ, our Lord. It is Jesus, our Lord and Savior, who communicates to us the graces that we need to unite ourselves with God. Our Lord said, "I am the way, and the truth, and the life. No one comes to the Father except through me" (Jn 14:6). Therefore, our Lord Jesus is *the* way to our sanctification.

The body of Christ exists naturally only in heaven, and sacramentally in the Eucharist. However, a holy person is constantly under the influence of our Lord's sacred humanity. It is from His humanity that we receive the graces that we need to live the life of God. Christ instituted the Holy Eucharist to be our constant source of life and strength. When we receive Holy Communion, we receive divine life directly from Him. This is why eminent theologians say that, as nothing is more desirable in the life hereafter than the beatific vision, so in the present life nothing can be more desirable than Holy Communion.[8]

As no one comes to the Father except through Christ Jesus, so no one comes to Jesus except through Mary. Jesus and Mary are the two anchors of our salvation and sanctification. Mary, in fact, is sometimes given the title of co-Redemptrix because she played such an active and important role in the redemption of humankind. And we must never forget that she is our spiritual mother, too.[9] As our Mother, she has a role in forming us. She dispenses God's graces and *transforms us into the likeness of Jesus.* This is why Saint Louis de Montfort, following Saint Augustine, appropriately called her

---

[8] See, for example, Reginald Garrigou-Lagrange, OP, *Christian Perfection and Contemplation,* tr. by Sister M. Timothea Doyle, OP (St. Louis, MO: B. Herder Book Co., 1946), Part III, Art. I, p. 58.

[9] See *The Catechism of the Catholic Church* (Liguori Publications, 1994), #968 and 969.

the living mould of God — *forma Dei.*[10]

Therefore, we must work closely with Mary if we want to come close to Jesus. All the great saints and mystics of the Catholic Church had a great devotion to the Mother of God. These include Saint Francis of Assisi, Saint Ignatius of Loyola, Saint Teresa of Avila and Saint John of the Cross.[11] Even the popular Saint Thérèse of Lisieux had a great devotion to the Blessed Virgin, to whom she attributed her recovery from a certain illness.[12] All these saints knew that true devotion to Mary ultimately leads to Christ. As St. Louis Grignon de Montfort affirmed, "Christ must be the ultimate end of all devotions."[13]

With respect to Mary's power of intercession, Saint Louis explained that in heaven Christ remains as much the Son of Mary as He was on earth. If this is true, then Christ must be subject to her authority as any good son is. Saint Louis explains:

---

[10] Saint Louis Marie Grignion de Montfort, *True Devotion to Mary*, Ch. 6, #219, as published in *God Alone: The Collected Writings of St. Louis Marie de Montfort* (Bay Shore, NY: Montfort Publications, 1987), p. 361.

[11] See Raphael Brown, *Saints Who Saw Mary* (Rockford, IL: TAN Books, 1994). This book was first published in 1955 by St. Meinrad's Archabbey, Inc.

[12] Cf. St. Thérèse of Lisieux, *The Story of a Soul,* tr. by John Beevers (Garden City, NY: Doubleday Image Books, 1957), Chapter 3.

[13] Saint Louis Marie Grignion de Montfort, *True Devotion to Mary,* Ch. 2, *op. cit.*, p. 307.

We must take care, however, not to consider this dependence as an abasement or imperfection in Jesus Christ. For Mary, infinitely inferior to her Son, who is God, does not command him in the same way as an earthly mother would command her child who is beneath her. Since she (Mary) is completely transformed in God by that grace and glory which transforms all the saints in him, *she does not ask or wish to do anything which is contrary to the eternal and unchangeable will of God.* When therefore we read in the writings of St. Bernard, St. Bernardine, St. Bonaventure, and others that all in heaven and on earth, even God himself, is subject to the Blessed Virgin, they mean that the authority which God was pleased to give her is so great that she seems to have the same power as God. Her prayers and requests are so powerful with him that he accepts them as commands *in the sense that he never resists his dear mother's prayer because it is always humble and conformed to his will.*[14] (Italics added)

We must emphasize that Saint Louis is not saying that God is subject to Mary *as if* Mary were more powerful than God Himself. Rather, *there is a perfect conformity between God's will and Mary's will,* and this is the basis of God's voluntary "subjection" to His mother's will.

In the same book Saint Louis implies that the devil fears Mary more than God — *not because* Mary

---

[14] *Ibid.*, Ch. 1, #27, p. 297.

is personally more powerful than God Himself but rather precisely *because she is infinitely far less powerful than God.* Because of his pride, the devil is infinitely more embarrassed to be defeated by a lowly virgin than by God.[15]

Therefore, let us not be scrupulous in our devotion to the Mother of God. Let us not think that we are offending God when we pray frequently to Mary, *as if* the final end of such devotion is not precisely to bring us closer to Jesus. Saint Louis notes that even the whole Catholic Church calls Mary blessed first, then Jesus in her prayer: "Blessed art thou among women and blessed is the fruit of thy womb, Jesus."[16] The Church's veneration of Mary above all saints is not an exaggeration, but the constant teaching of the Catholic Church. The Fathers of the Second Vatican Council honored Mary, not merely as a model of the Church and, indeed, her Mother, but especially as the *Mother of God Himself*, which she truly is. Like Saint Alphonsus de Liguori, they did not hesitate to proclaim her glory. "Because of this gift of sublime grace," Vatican II says, "she (Mary) surpasses all other creatures, *both in heaven and on earth.*"[17]

---

[15] *Op. cit.,* Ch. 1, #52, pp. 304-305.

[16] *Op. cit.,* Ch. 2, #95, p. 319

[17] Vatican II, *Dogmatic Constitution on the Church (Lumen Gentium),* #53, as translated in *The Documents of Vatican II,* ed. by Walter M. Abbott and Joseph Gallagher (America Press, 1966), p. 86. (Italics added.)

Chapter 2

THE MAKING OF A SAINT

Growing in Perfection

Our spiritual growth reflects our progress in the friendship of God. The life of grace and charity is never static but ever dynamic. It grows continually until our death. This is how it should be, for friendship admits of no repose or laziness. It is a law that, in the way of love, one must always advance in order not to fall back.[1] A person who does not advance in charity suffers the penalty of becoming a spiritually retarded soul.

It is tragic at times to find people who, after spending many years in spiritual exercises, still find themselves very far from perfection. They remain, as it were, "spiritual dwarfs." Because of their lukewarmness or their mediocre devotion, they fail to advance in Christian perfection. Spiritual life should not be like this. Rather, the life of charity should grow steadily in us with little or no interruption. The more the love of God increases, the more rapidly it should still grow, just as a falling body increases its speed the closer it gets to the ground.[2] The Book of Proverbs expresses this doctrine very clearly: "The path of the righteous is like

---

[1] John Tauler, *Institutions,* Ch. 34.

[2] See Saint Thomas Aquinas, *Summa Contra Gentiles,* Book I, Ch. 91, No. 5.

the light of dawn which shines brighter and brighter until it is full day" (Pr 4:18). Among the saints charity becomes more intense with age.

The trouble is that we often do not persevere when we are getting into difficulty. We stop advancing, become tepid, and eventually fall back. But we should never give up. In the long run those who succeed in this struggle are not the ones who never fall, but those who never cease getting up again and starting all over after each fall.

Theologians distinguish three stages in the spiritual life: the age of the *beginner,* the age of the *proficient,* and the age of the *perfect.* Let me explain each stage briefly.

The Age of the Beginner

In this stage the prayer of the aspirant consists mostly of *meditation,* where reason and imagination play a dominant role. The aspirant mortifies his body and his soul to liberate the spirit from all forms of bodily and spiritual attachments. The necessity of these mortifications was indicated by our Lord: "Amen, amen I say to you, if the grain of wheat that falls to the ground does not die, it remains alone. But if it dies, it bears much fruit" (Jn 12:23-24). Saint Paul also said, "Put to death those parts of you which are earthly... strip away the old man with his deeds and put on the new one which is being renewed according to the image of its Creator" (Col 3:5, 9-10).

Normally, a person in this stage cannot proceed to the next stage, that is, to the stage of the proficient, unless God Himself helps to purify him. This purification is the "night of the senses" that Saint John of the Cross spoke about.[3] God Himself is the one who performs this purification: "I am the true vine; and my Father is the vinedresser. Every branch in me not bearing fruit, He will remove. And every one bearing fruit, He will prune so that it will bring forth more fruit" (Jn 15:1-2). He accomplishes this by permitting temptations to come to the aspirant, and by allowing misfortunes to fall on him, so that he may cling to Him more ardently.

Saint John of the Cross mentions three signs of these passive purifications:

1. Aridity and dryness of the spirit. God deprives the beginner of any sensible sweetness in prayer and other spiritual exercises. The beginner suffers the absence of any comfort in material as well as spiritual things, including spiritual readings and instruction.
2. The anxiety of being separated from God. The

---

[3] See Saint John of the Cross, *The Dark Night of the Soul,* Book I. Tr. by Kieran Kavanaugh, OCD and Otilio Rodriguez, OCD in *The Collected Works of St. John of the Cross* (Washington, DC: ICS Publications, 1973 paperback edition).

beginner becomes painfully anxious that he is no longer serving God, although he keeps a keen desire to serve Him and a strong resolution to resist temptations. His aridity is not the same as lukewarmness. The arid beginner suffers precisely because he is ready and willing to serve God. But because of the absence of sensible consolations and sweetness in his prayers, he feels that he is no longer doing so.

3. Inability to meditate and a facility to maintain a simple, loving gaze. There is a change in the manner of his prayer. He finds it increasingly difficult to pray by making use of words and images. He feels more comfortable in a kind of prayer that consists merely in a quiet and restful contemplation of God's presence.

The Age of the Proficient

In this stage the aspirant becomes zealous in performing good works, such as praying, teaching, caring for the sick, *etc.* He does not merely avoid sin, but also practices the virtues. He receives from God an increase in the gifts of knowledge, understanding, wisdom, fear and piety. He comes to know God more, not by reading or meditation, but through the lights he receives in prayer. His prayer is no longer discursive, as meditation is, but simply affective.

Theologians here distinguish two grades of affective prayer. First, there is the *passive prayer of recollection* by which the aspirant, without any labor of his own, penetrates the mysteries of salvation. He performs this without using imagination, reasoning or meditation. The prayer simply consists in a union of the mind and heart with God, which is characterized by a certain "suspension of the soul." This is nothing else than a perfect attention to God and an utter forgetfulness of everything else. Strictly speaking, this state cannot be acquired by one's efforts alone. Human efforts are powerless to attain it. At best a person can only prepare himself to receive such grace, which God generously gives to those who sincerely seek Him. Those on whom God confers this grace acquire a superior knowledge, an intuition as it were, of God's intimate life. This knowledge is so profound that they, by their efforts alone, would not have obtained it even with years of study and meditation. Yet this is only the lowest degree of affective-contemplative prayer.

The second grade of affective prayer is the *prayer of quiet,* which consists in a union of the will with God. In this prayer God sets the heart afire, making the proficient experience such ineffable "delights" that all the soul's faculties are held still.

Saint Teresa of Jesus explains that this spiritual consolation produces in the most intimate depths of the soul the greatest peace, tranquility and sweetness.[4] However, this is again a heavenly favor that cannot be obtained by any effort of our own. It is God Himself who freely confers this gift on those whom He wills, and often at a time when the aspirant least expects it. This is why "delight" is *not* the same as the "satisfaction" that one ordinarily feels in performing a good meditation or some good act. One can obtain satisfaction at will, but delight, no. Like the prayer of recollection, the prayer of quiet has some beneficial effects. It gives spiritual strength to the soul, and the facility to perform good deeds. The aspirant experiences peace, joy, and a holy zeal to serve God more.

Notwithstanding these gifts, the aspirant at this stage still has many imperfections. Sometimes a secret pride lurks behind his zeal and good intentions to teach or to perform works of mercy. Sometimes he acquires a spiritual gluttony for the consolations he receives in prayer. He may be quite in earnest in the practice of virtue, but a subtle egoism often makes him perform spiritual acts in a manner that is not yet sufficiently detached.

He cannot purify himself of these defects

---

[4] Saint Teresa of Jesus, *Interior Castle* (Garden City, NY: Doubleday Image Books, 1961), Fourth Mansion, Chapter II. Tr. by E. Allison Peers.

unless God helps him. By his efforts alone, the aspirant cannot enter the age of the perfect. God has to put him through another type of purification, the more painful and darker "night of the spirit" that Saint John of the Cross spoke about.[5] Words cannot express, Saint Thérèse of Lisieux says, the darkness into which the soul is plunged during the night of the spirit.[6] One has to pass through it himself to understand it. Sometimes the aspirant is tempted against faith. At other times he feels himself completely abandoned.[7] Tauler says that often the Holy Spirit creates a *void* in the depths of the soul where, in the midst of his sufferings, the aspirant realizes his nothingness before God. This kills his secret egoism and pride.[8] There are also cases when God allows the aspirant to be possessed by the devil, if only to make him realize his helplessness without Him.[9] But, no matter how difficult, it is precisely in this night of the spirit that

---

[5] See Saint John of the Cross, *The Dark Night of the Soul,* Book II.

[6] Saint Thérèse of Lisieux, *The Story of a Soul,* Ch. 9.

[7] Saint Paul of the Cross, *Letters,* I, 153.

[8] Tauler, *Second Sermon for Pentecost.*

[9] Cases of diabolical possession have been noted in the lives of the Curé d'Ars, Saint Margaret of Cortona, Saint Veronica Giuliani, Sister Josefa Menéndez, and many others. In all these cases the action of the devil does not go beyond the sensible part of the soul and does not hinder the free use of the intellect and the will. Many of the saints were even known to blaspheme *without their willing it.* However, even in the most violent state when the devil had full control of the body, their will remained immutably fixed in God.

the soul is purified. The aspirant apprehends more clearly his indigence and wretchedness, and in contrast, God's majesty and goodness.

The Age of the Perfect

Coming from the dark night of the spirit, the aspirant finally enters the age of the perfect. Saint Teresa now compares the aspirant to a silkworm that comes out of its cocoon as a beautiful butter-fly.[10] At this stage the aspirant lives as though God Himself lives in him.[11] He walks with a *consciousness* of God's presence. He engages frequently in *contemplation* as his proper mode of prayer. Often this contemplation is *infused,* for God Himself is its author. By this prayer, he rises above the multiplicity of sensible images and ideas. Under the inspiration of the Holy Spirit, he unites himself to God in a sweet and loving relationship.

Contemplation is an advanced form of affective prayer. It is not specifically distinct from the affective prayer practiced by the proficients. In affective prayer, however, one merely penetrates the mysteries of salvation. But in contemplation one penetrates the Essence of God Himself. Through

---

[10] Saint Teresa of Jesus, *Interior Castle,* Fifth Mansion, Chapter II.

[11] "It is no longer *I* who live; but it is Christ who lives in me" — Saint Paul (Gal 2:20).

contemplation the aspirant acquires a familiarity with the Three Divine Persons. With them he engages in sweet yet silent conversations.

This does not mean that the perfect no longer perform the prayer of recollection and the prayer of quiet, which characterize the prayer of the proficient. They still do, but above these lower grades of prayer are other more exalted forms of prayer that God grants only to the perfect. Theologians here distinguish two grades of prayer. The first is the *prayer of simple union,* so called because it consists in a union of all the faculties with God. Because it consists in a certain contact with God Himself, it has been called by several names, such as "unction," "kiss," "perfume," "heavenly dew," *etc.* In the prayer of simple union all the faculties remain united to God who holds them captive, the soul experiencing a certain "sleep" or "ecstasy." This is an actual sleep. As Saint Teresa of Jesus explains, "for the short time that the condition lasts, the soul is without consciousness and has no power to think, even though it may desire to do so."[12] Saint Thérèse of Lisieux refers to it as "the living death." During this brief duration God establishes Himself in the interior of the soul, and makes so deep an impression that the experience cannot be forgotten even

---

[12] Saint Teresa of Jesus, *Interior Castle*, Fifth Mansion, Chapter I, p. 97.

after many years have passed. Neither can the subject doubt that he has been visited and "kissed" by God. The effects of the prayer of union are quite helpful. The mystic feels a strong desire to love God more ardently, suffer great trials and undertake the most severe penances.

The second grade of contemplative prayer during this stage of the perfect is the *prayer of transforming union.* This begins with the "mystical engagement" and culminates in the "mystical marriage." In this stage the prayer is "transforming" because it "deifies" the saint and makes him one with God Himself. It begins when our Lord and the saint enter into an engagement by which they promise themselves solemnly to each other. Sometimes our Lord gives the saint an engagement ring. He gave one to Saint Catherine of Siena, which was always visible but to her only. Saint Catherine de Ricci also received a ring that was visible even to others.[13] However, mystical engagement is not the end, but the preliminary step to a more exalted state, which is mystical marriage. In this stage God becomes the bridegroom of the soul. The saint lives more by the Divine Life in him than by the human life that he naturally has. Now God and the saint are mystically one.

---

[13] See Fr. John Arintero, OP, *Mystical Evolution* (Rockford, IL: TAN Books, 1978), Vol. II, Chapter 5, p. 170 at the footnote.

Reaching the Ultimate Goal

Saint John of the Cross says that there are many who reach the gate of perfection, but only a few actually enter it. By this he means that only a few actually enter the stage of the perfect because the dedication required for this state is total and complete, and only a few are willing to make the sacrifice. But God demands nothing less than total love as a necessary condition for mystical union.[14] In the realm of love God admits no rival. He makes no compromises for His love is a love of *friendship*. He wants His beloved to be nothing less that His *other self*. This is why Saint John of the Cross said that to love God it is necessary to strip oneself *of everything that is not God*.

To be united with God, the aspirant should have no other desire but God Himself. He should have no attachment to anything, not even to the delights of prayer and the satisfaction of performing good works. A person who prays and performs acts of mercy because of the pleasure and satisfaction he derives from them, is still very far from reaching God. He must be detached from spiritual satisfactions and delights, and must seek only God

---

[14] Many theologians of the spiritual life hold that there is no exception to this rule. Even those who die in the state of grace, but who fail to attain mystical union in this life, have to be purified in purgatory before they can enter heaven. "Nothing impure will enter it" (Rv 21:27). Our Lord Jesus also said that no one will enter the Kingdom until he has repaid "the last penny" (Mt 5:26).

Himself, if he wishes to be united with Him in this way. This means that a person must be ready to give up even a delightful state of prayer if duty or charity so requires. Blessed Henry Suso says that he who does not know how to leave God for God will be abandoned by God.[15]

Saint John of the Cross explains that our little attachments to creatures (which include spiritual pleasures) hinder us from reaching God:

> It makes little difference whether a bird is tied by a thin thread or by a cord. For even if tied by thread, the bird will be prevented from taking off just as surely as if it were tied by cord — that is, it will be impeded from flight as long as it does not break the thread... This is the lot of a man who is attached to something; no matter how much virtue he has he will not reach the freedom of the divine union.[16]

Saint John of the Cross deplores the fact that many fail to reach the summit of spiritual perfection because they fail to break the last thin cord that holds them back. Yet, the love of God will not have it in any other way, for God wants us to belong totally to Him. It is only in this total love that our hearts will find true rest.

---

[15] Blessed Henry Suso, *Union,* Ch. 3.

[16] Saint John of the Cross, *Ascent of Mount Carmel,* Book I, Ch. XI, #4. Tr. by Kieran Kavanaugh, OCD and Otilio Rodriguez, OCD in *The Collected Works of St. John of the Cross* (Washington, DC: ICS Publications, 1973), p. 97.

CHAPTER 3

MYSTICISM AND WISDOM

The Wisdom of the Sage

There are two ways of knowing God — the conceptual way and the non-conceptual way. The conceptual way is the method of the sage, the philosopher or the theologian, who employs logic and reasoning to form concepts of God and heavenly things. The non-conceptual way is the method of the saints, who attain an intimate knowledge of God by love.

The science of the sage is twofold. There is, first, the kind of science attained solely by the exercise of reason without the aid of divine revelation. This culminates in *metaphysical wisdom,* the wisdom of the philosopher. By reasoning from principles derived from the world of common experience, the philosopher forms concepts about God as First Cause of all reality. The philosopher knows God, not as He is in Himself, but as He is manifested by the things that He has made.

Next, there is a science of God attained by faith in divine revelation. By reasoning from principles derived from divine revelation, one can attain a science of God, not as revealed by creatures, but as revealed by God Himself. By faith one attains a knowledge of God's intimate life, *but without actually seeing Him.* This knowledge results in *theological wisdom.* By faith in God's word, the theologian constructs a rational *science* of God that is otherwise inaccessible to human reason.

Because the philosopher and the theologian employ logic and reasoning in forming their concepts of God, their science is necessarily conceptual and rational. But, to the extent that their science is *of* God, or the ultimate reality, their science is properly called "wisdom." Yet, this wisdom is inferior to the science of the Blessed, who also know God, not by study and reasoning, nor by simply believing Him, but by actually *seeing* Him. In heaven the saints enjoy a direct vision of the Divine Essence.

God is above reason. In this life, therefore, a perfect, rationally constructed knowledge of God is impossible because the Divine Being cannot be represented adequately by any concept. Every conceptual knowledge that we have is of something that is *not* God. So, by the conceptual method alone both the philosopher and the theologian can only describe God by what He is not, rather than by what He is. For example, when the philosopher or the theologian describes God as *infinite,* what he means is that God is not a limited being.

Since the Divine Essence transcends all human sciences and all reasoning, therefore the perfect knowledge of God is *beyond* philosophy and *beyond* theology. Still, this twofold wisdom, each in its own order, may be regarded as the highest point of *rational* accomplishment in the present life.

The Wisdom of the Saint

There is one other way of knowing God in this life that is better than the way of the philosopher or that of the theologian. This is the non-conceptual way of the mystics and the saints. The mystics attain a knowledge of God, not by study and reasoning, but by love. Philosophers and religious thinkers have long recognized the existence of this kind of non-conceptual knowledge. For example, they know that even without so many words and reasoning, people understand better the things that they love. "The heart has its reasons, which reason does not know," says Pascal.[1] More recently, Antoine de Saint-Exupéry also says, "It is only with the heart that one can see rightly."[2]

The formal effect of love is to unite, so that the lover and the beloved, while remaining distinct as entities, become somehow "one." When a person is united to God by charity, he acquires a bet-

---

[1] Blaise Pascal, *Pensées,* Section IV, Par. 277. Tr. by W.F. Trotter in Vol. 33 of *Great Books of the Western World* (Encyclopedia Britannica, 1952), p. 222.

[2] Antoine de Saint-Exupéry, *The Little Prince,* tr. by Katherine Woods (Penguin Books, 1962), p. 84.

ter understanding of God, which is the result, not of long study and philosophical reasoning, but of the affective union itself. Saint Thomas Aquinas speaks of this understanding as the result of a certain "connaturality" with the object loved.[3]

This is how the mystic knows God better than the most learned philosopher or theologian. The philosopher knows God only by what He is not and in the mirror of the things that He has made, whereas the mystic or the saint knows God *as He is in Himself,* as the object of his love. The saint also knows God better than any speculative theologian. For, although the theologian derives his science from truths revealed by God Himself, he knows God only *objectively,* that is, as the object of a concept. But by his heart, the saint knows God *subjectively,* that is, by becoming intimately one with God, Who is his Friend.

In the friendship that they enjoy with God, the saints in this life know their Friend subjectively but certainly. This knowledge may not be as clear as the Beatific Vision that the Blessed in heaven enjoy. But subjectively it is far more certain and delightful than any rationally constructed science attained with or without the aid of divine revelation. Like the sage, the saint knows the ultimate

---

[3] Saint Thomas Aquinas, *Summa Theologiae ,* II-II, q. 45, art. 4.

reality. But unlike the sage, the saint attains this wisdom, not by way of concepts and discursive reasoning, but by a sort of "contact" with the divine.

For the sage, wisdom is an acquired virtue of the speculative intellect. For the saint, it is an infused gift of the Holy Spirit, the highest of the seven gifts.[4] By means of this gift the saint, like the sage but better than the sage, learns the "deep things of God,"[5] the things that God reveals to the simple but hides from the wise.[6]

Therefore, a mystic is literally a saint on earth, a person who loves God and whom God loves in return. Friendship unites him to God by a conformity of wills, such that he wills whatever God wills. Long ago Aristotle described a friend as a person's "other self."[7] This is exactly how God the Father spoke of His friends to Saint Catherine of Siena: "So I say, if you should ask me who they are, I would answer... that they are another me; for they have lost and drowned their own will and have clothed themselves and united themselves and conformed themselves with mine."[8]

---

[4] See the Book of Wisdom 7:7-28.

[5] 1 Cor 2:10.

[6] Mt 11:25.

[7] Aristotle, *Nicomachean Ethics,* Book IX, Ch. 4, 1166a32.

[8] Catherine of Siena, *The Dialogue,* tr. by Suzanne Noffke (New York: Paulist Press, 1980), Prologue, p. 26. This edition belongs to *The Classics of Western Spirituality* series.

But mystical friendship is more than a union of wills. It is a union of *life* itself and almost a union of natures. Saint Paul says, "It is no longer I who live; it is Christ who lives in me" (Gal 2:20). It is amazing how this could be, since in mystical union God and the soul remain *distinct* as entities. And yet the two are so united by charity that they seem to live the same life. God and the saint are no longer discernible apart. As Saint John of the Cross says, "The intellect of this soul is God's intellect; its will is God's will; its memory is the memory of God; and its delight is God's delight."[9]

In his union with God the mystic does not merely participate in God's exterior works, but even feels the impulses, or the inner life and acts of the Divine Persons.[10] This is how he knows and understands God better than the most learned, speculative theologian. By faith the theologian also knows God according to what He is, since it is God Himself who reveals Himself to us. But in communicating Himself, God employs the medium of human language and human concepts. So the

---

[9] Saint John of the Cross, *The Living Flame of Love,* Stanza 2, Commentary 34. Tr. by Kieran Kavanaugh, OCD and Otilio Rodriguez, OCD in *The Collected Works of St. John of the Cross* (Washington, DC: ICS Publications, 1973), p. 608.

[10] The Gospel of Saint John 14:23 reveals the indwelling of the Blessed Trinity in the souls of the just. Pope Leo XIII explained this in his encyclical *Divinum illud munus,* May 9, 1897.

theologian's knowledge, certain and infallible though it be, is to that extent, still negative. It is a knowledge of what God is not. Unlike the theologian who knows God only by faith and by means of concepts, the mystic in a way *experiences* God by love. Through this love he knows God, not merely as represented in a concept, but as a present reality whose companionship he enjoys.

A mystic, whose will is one with God, no longer acts "according to the rules of right reason." Through the gifts of the Holy Spirit he actually becomes passive and wholly responsive to the promptings of the Holy Spirit.[11] He lives not so much through the active exercise of his powers and freedom, but on the initiative and action of God Himself. Saint Gregory Nazianzen aptly compares him to "a musical instrument vibrated by the Spirit, proclaiming in melody, the divine power and glory."[12]

At the same time, however, the mystic remains fully free and truly independent. The slightest movement of his will is significant, since it

---

[11] "In the gifts of the Holy Ghost," Saint Thomas says, "the position of the human mind is of one moved rather than of a mover." See *Summa Theologiae* , Part II-II, q. 52, art. 2, Reply to Obj. 1. Tr. by the Fathers of the English Dominican Province in *Summa Theologica* (Benziger Brothers, Inc.: 1947), Vol. II, p. 1413.

[12] Quoted by Father John G. Arintero, *Mystical Evolution* (Rockford, IL: TAN Books, 1978), Vol. I, Introduction, p. 3, in the footnote.

reflects the Divine Will. Here on earth the saints can judge moral and divine matters better than philosophers or theologians. This is because they are, by love, "co-natured" with Goodness Itself, the final end of all human acts.[13] They only have to examine their inclinations to know what God wills, or what is good and just. They may not be able to justify their judgment rationally, but they are *certain* of the truth of their judgment. Theirs is a mode of knowing that is non-conceptual and non-rational. Yet it is *not* irrational, and is superior to the rational mode of knowing employed by the philosophers.

Reality and Metaphor

Like any other experience, mystical experience is essentially indescribable. The mystical knowledge of God is to the inexperienced soul what the science of optics is to the blind. The natural, human mode of knowing takes place by means of concepts, whereas the mystical mode of knowing happens precisely in the absence of such concepts. Nobody knows exactly how this is accomplished. However, the cumulative testimony of the saints

---

[13] Saint Thomas Aquinas, *Summa Theologiae,* II-II, q. 45, art. 2 and 4.

and the mystics, who had the privilege of experiencing this special mode of knowing, suggests that the human mind is more fertile than we know. Although naturally discursive, the human mind is open to the work of grace. To those of us who have never enjoyed this sublime experience, mystical knowledge will remain a mystery, and will be as much an object of faith as grace is.

Precisely because the knowledge of the mystics is non-conceptual, the mystics have a difficulty in using words (or concepts) to describe their experiences to others. Even the fluent Saint Teresa of Avila seems to be groping for words in describing her experiences. For instance, she says:

> This satisfaction resides in the most intimate part of the soul, and the soul cannot tell whence or how it has come to it; often it knows neither what to do, nor to wish, nor to ask. It seems to find everything at once, yet not to know what it has found: I do not myself know how to explain this.[14]

Saint Catherine of Siena, another woman Doctor of the Church, seems to suffer the same predicament. She would rather not talk about her spiri-

---

[14] Saint Teresa of Jesus, *The Autobiography of Saint Teresa of Jesus,* tr. by E. Allison Peers (Garden City, NY: Image Books, 1960), Ch. XIV, p. 150.

tual experiences: "I would feel that I had *blasphemed.*"[15]

The person who attains this obscure knowledge — which is attained by "unknowing," yet transcending all forms of knowing — becomes somehow mute. He cannot describe his experiences except in ciphers and symbols. But, although not possessing the precision of philosophical language, the metaphorical language employed by the mystic is more fitting and more *exact* because of the loftiness of the experience that it conveys. For the mystic, metaphor is not a rhetorical device, but a manner of speaking that is proportionate to the reality that it describes. The mystic has no better way of describing an experience that has no counterpart in sensible experience, and which is wholly *above,* and *uncaught* by, our distinct concepts.

Philosophers define reality by giving their concept of it, while the mystics have to describe reality by communicating their experience of it. It is only by experiencing it that the hearers can understand it. The language of the philosophers and the theologians are practically useless, and even self-defeating, in describing an experience that is

---

[15] Saint Catherine of Siena, *Autobiography,* II, Part VI (Italics added). Quoted by John G. Arintero in *The Mystical Evolution.* Tr. by Fr. Jordan Aumann, OP (Rockford, IL: TAN Books and Publishers, Inc. 1978), Vol. II, Part III, Ch. VII, p. 320.

essentially incapable of exact description by words and ideas. Their technical terms and procedures only arrest those loving impulses that are the primary content of all mystical experiences. Using metaphorical language, for example, our Lord invited those who seek eternal life to approach him, saying: "The water that I shall give him, shall become in him a fountain of water, springing up into life everlasting" (Jn 4:14). Fr. Garrigou-Lagrange wisely noted that it is doubtful if our Lord would have been better understood if He had employed theological jargon in making this invitation.[16] The expression would have been something like this: "The *habitus* of sanctifying grace that I shall give him, shall become in him the source of the infused virtues and gifts of the Holy Spirit."

In reading their writings, therefore, we must give the mystics some indulgence when they use metaphor to describe reality. In expressing the worthlessness of creatures before God, for example, the mystics might say that creatures are *nothing*. They were right. Creatures are as "nothing" compared to God, although not nothing in the ontological sense of the term.

---

[16] See Reginald Garrigou-Lagrange, *The Three Ages of the Interior Life*. Tr. by Sister M. Timothea Doyle, OP (Rockford, IL: TAN Books and Publishers, Inc., 1989), Vol. II, Part III, Ch. I, pp. 19-20.

Likewise, the mystic might describe contemplation as the *absence of all action,* whereas the philosopher describes it as the *highest human activity.* In spite of this difference, they are in perfect accord. The philosopher is speaking from the metaphysical standpoint, according to which there can be no higher activity than this immanent operation of knowing and loving God. But the saint is speaking from the standpoint of mystical experience. Since the contemplation of God is accompanied by the suspension of all activities of a human mode, it does appear to the saint as the absence of all action.[17]

One must bear this in mind when reading the writings of the great mystics of the Church. A superficial reading of Christian mystical literature might give the impression that the Christian mystics are pantheists and idolaters. Since human language cannot perfectly describe the intimate union of their soul with God, the mystics seem at times to identify themselves with the Creator. However, they are neither pantheists nor idolaters. The statements of the Christian mystics are entirely different from the affirmations of the Eastern religions.

---

[17] See Jacques Maritain, *The Degrees of Knowledge,* tr. from the fourth edition under the supervision of Gerald B. Phelan (New York: Charles Scribner's Sons, 1959), Part II, Ch. 8, p. 327.

Mysticism and Hindu Philosophy

By way of an illustration, let me compare the affirmations of the saints with those found, for example, in the *Upanishads*. Unlike Christian mystical wisdom, Hindu philosophy is truly *pantheistic*. It sees the universe as an outpouring or emanation of Brahman, the Universal Consciousness. For example, we read in the *Khandogya-Upanishad:*

> 'In the beginning,' my dear, 'there was that only which is (*tò o on*), one only, without a second...'
>
> 'It thought, may I be many, may I grow forth. It sent forth fire.'
>
> 'That fire thought, may I be many, may I grow forth. It sent forth water...'
>
> 'Water thought, may I be many, may I grow forth. It sent forth earth (food).'
>
> 'That Being (i.e., that which had produced fire, water, and earth) thought, let me now enter those three beings (fire, water, earth) with this living Self (*giva atma*), and let me then reveal (develop) names and forms.'[18]

So, in the beginning there was only Brahman, one being "without a second." Then, "It thought," in-

---

[18] *Khandogya-Upanishad,* VI Prapathaka, 2 and 3 Khanda. Tr. by various Oriental scholars and edited by F. Max Müller in *The Upanishads,* (New York: Dover Publications, Inc., 1962), Part I, pp. 93-95.

dicating that Brahman was a conscious being. Eventually Brahman emanated into fire, then water, then earth.[19] Finally, Brahman entered as a living Self into the composition of all things. "He (Brahman or the Self) entered thither, to the very tips of the finger-nails...."[20] So, Brahman is *immanent* in all things. If we give Brahman the name "God," then in Hindu philosophy God is in all things, and everything is God.

According to this philosophy, man himself is divine. He who becomes profoundly conscious of this fact, becomes Brahman:

> Verily in the beginning this was Brahman, that Brahman knew (its) Self only, saying, 'I am Brahman.' From it all this sprang. Thus, whatever Deva was awakened (so as to know Brahman), he indeed became that (Brahman); and the same with Rishis and men. The Rishi Vamadeva saw and understood it, singing, 'I was Manu (moon),

---

[19] Surprisingly, these are the same elements that the ancient Greek philosophers regard as the primary stuff of the universe. Of course, the Greeks also include air as one of the elements. In the *Khandogya-Upanishads* air was left out probably because the Hindus already identified air with Brahman. Thus, we read in another Upanishad text, "Adoration to thee, O Vayu (air)! Thou indeed art the visible Brahman." — *Taittiriyaka-Upanishad,* I Valli, 1 Anuvaka. Tr. in *The Upanishads,* Part II, p. 45.

[20] *Brihadaranyaka-Upanishad,* I Adhyaya, 4 Brahmana. Tr. in *The Upanishads,* Part II, p. 87.

> I was the sun.' Therefore now also he who thus knows that he is Brahman, becomes all this, and even the Devas cannot prevent it, for he himself is their Self.[21]

Therefore, the main effort of a Hindu "mystic" is concentrated on knowing the Self, and in realizing that he himself *is* Brahman. Now, this is entirely different from the thoughts of the Christian mystics. If the Christians seem to identify themselves with God, it is only because of the limitations of our language, which is unable to describe realities beyond the contents of our concepts and perceptions. The Christian mystics are aware that such images as the light from two candles joined into one, or the metaphor of water from a stream that joins the sea, are very imperfect descriptions of the union of their soul with God.[22] No matter how united to God they may be, the Christians remain conscious of the *distinction* between their human nature and the divine nature. They are aware that they are *not* God; otherwise, they will not realize their nothingness before Him.

In Christianity, of course, God is also immanent in all things. However, God is not in all things

---

[21] *Ibid,* p. 88.

[22] Cf. Saint Teresa of Jesus, *The Interior Castle,* Seventh Mansion, Ch. 2.

as a *material cause,* but as an *efficient cause.*[23] As such, God is *distinct* from the world and *transcends* it. For the Christian, God is immanent in the world because God continually preserves its being. Since every cause *as causing* must be present in its effect, so God as cause of being must be continually present in His creatures.[24]

In contrast, pantheists think that Brahman is the "stuff" of the universe, and that they themselves are gods. For Christians to see the world in this manner is totally dangerous. It reduces mysticism to idolatry. To borrow the phraseology of Cardinal Mercier of Brussels, Christians who think this way end up in a kind of "misty schism." Instead of becoming genuine mystics, they become genuine "mistakes," exposing themselves to great danger in the vain attempt to identify themselves and all things with the Creator.

Creatures can never be gods by nature. However, there is one sense in which Christians can

---

[23] A *cause* is anything that contributes to the production of an effect. The question, "What is the cause of this table?" requires many answers. The cause of the table is not merely the craftsman who made the table. The craftsman is the *efficient cause* — for without his activity the table cannot be made. But the wood, out of which the table is made, is also a cause. Without it, the table also cannot be made. Unlike the craftsman, however, which is extrinsic to the table itself, the wood is an intrinsic, *material cause* because it enters into the composition and being of the table itself.

[24] See Saint Thomas Aquinas, *Summa Theologiae* , Part I, q. 8, art. 1.

truly call themselves "children of God," not by nature but by *grace*. For example, the *Catechism of the Catholic Church* says that by the grace of baptism we become adopted "sons of God" and "partakers of the divine nature."[25] Now, this divine sonship is not just a metaphorical sonship similar to human adoption. This sonship is a *real* sonship, the result of our nature being elevated by grace to share in the life of God Himself.

Philosophy and the Christian Idea of "Deification"

To show why the Christian idea of deification is quite different from that of the pantheist, let me explain more fully in what sense God and the soul are said by Christians to be "one." It is impossible by reason alone to figure out how a finite being can ever become one with the Infinite God, or share in His life. The possibility of grace, or a creature's participation in the life of God, cannot be proved by reason. We learn it only from divine revelation. It was revealed when Saint John the Evangelist said that we shall see God *as He is.*[26] Clearly the Evangelist must be speaking of an *intellectual* vision, for

---

[25] *The Catechism of the Catholic Church,* #1265. Also, 1 Peter 1:4.
[26] 1 Jn 3:32.

God cannot be seen by our bodily eyes. But, since our nature by itself cannot attain to an immediate knowledge of the Infinite God, it must be by the elevation of human nature by grace that the saints enjoy a direct knowledge of the Divine Essence.[27] By the light of glory granted to the saints, the saints see God face to face. And in this knowledge they become "one" with God Himself, not in the order of substance, but in that other order of being by which the knower and the known become one.

The philosophy of human cognition helps to clarify how saints, by their vision of the Divine Essence, become "one" with God without being absorbed into the Unity of the Infinite Being. For, how does a knower know an object? To know an object, the knower must somehow possess the object, or become one with the object known, without the knower losing its own nature or its natural mode of being. Otherwise, the knower will not truly know the object, but will possess the object only by ceasing to be a knower. To be known, likewise, an object must somehow exist in and for the knower, and become one with the knower's act of knowing, without itself losing its natural mode of

---

[27] This is why Saint Thomas insists that the happiness of the saints consists in an act of the intellect by which the Blessed see God "face to face." According to Saint Thomas, eternal love results from this knowledge, and from this love eternal delight.

existing. Otherwise, the object will not be known, but will only be assimilated and transformed into the substance of the knower. For knowledge to be possible, therefore, there has to be another mode of being in which the knower and the known, while remaining distinct substances according to their natural mode of existing, become somehow one. Philosophers call this new mode of being *intentional,* to distinguish it from the *entitative* mode of being that things have in nature.

Knowledge, therefore, is a new mode of being. It is an act by which the knower and the known, while remaining distinct as entities, become intentionally one in the knower's *act* of knowing. This distinction between the entitative and the intentional mode of being in the philosophy of human cognition also solves the metaphysical problem regarding the union of the finite creature with the Infinite God. When the Christian says that through the Beatific Vision the saint is "divinized," or that the saint becomes "one" with God Himself, he does not mean that the saint's nature is stretched to infinity or is destroyed and absorbed into God's infinite nature. What he means is that in the very act of seeing God face to face the saint, while remaining substantially distinct from God's nature, becomes formally "one" with Him according to an *intentional* mode of being.

On earth those who are in the state of grace

do not see God face to face as the Blessed in heaven do. But they, too, are divinized when they love God with the love of *charity*. For love, like knowledge, also unites the lover with the beloved according to an intentional mode of being. In the act of loving and in being loved, the beloved exists (intentionally) in the heart of the person loving without either one losing its natural mode of being. The mystics who, through faith, love God with their whole heart, and whom God loves as His friends, become *intentionally,* though not substantially, "one" with God. This love is essentially the same as the charity that the Blessed in heaven have. The difference is that the love of God on earth results from faith, whereas among the Blessed the love of God results from the direct vision of the Divine Essence. Still, it is the same charity that makes one heart of two.

As grace is necessary for the Beatific Vision, so it is also necessary for charity. Without grace, it is impossible for us to obtain a love of friendship with God. With grace, however, the created soul is proportionately elevated for a special relationship where, in the love that they have for each other, God and the human person, while remaining distinct as substances, become intentionally one.

CHAPTER 4

THE MISSION OF THE SAINTS

Contemplation

Contemplation is the proper prayer of the saints. In this prayer the saint talks familiarly to God, and God in turn reveals Himself to him or her. But let us not have any misconceptions about this. Contemplation is neither a trance nor an ecstasy. It does not consist in a vision or in the hearing of strange words. God sometimes grants these extraordinary favors to a person, but they do not constitute contemplation as such.

What, then, is contemplation? Following Saint Thomas Aquinas, Fr. Reginald Garrigou-Lagrange defines contemplation as *"a simple, intellectual view of the truth, above reasoning and accompanied by admiration."*[1] In this sense, the simple vision of reality that a philosopher attains at the end of his study, is contemplation. Likewise, the loving knowledge of God as the principle and end of all things, attained by a theologian through faith, is contemplation. But this kind of contemplation is better termed "acquired contemplation," not only because it is acquired by a person's efforts, but to

---

[1] Reginald Garrigou-Lagrange, *The Three Ages of the Interior Life,* tr. by Sister M. Timothea Doyle, OP (Rockford, IL: TAN Books, 1989), Vol. II, Ch. 31, p. 309.

distinguish it from a specifically different kind of contemplation: the contemplation practiced by the saints. The contemplation by the mystics and the saints is "infused contemplation." It is a simple and loving knowledge of God that is not due to our personal effort, but to the special enlightenment by God Himself. Saint John of the Cross defines it as the inflowing of God into the soul whereby "God teaches the soul secretly and instructs it in the perfection of love without its doing anything nor understanding how it happens."[2] In other words, infused contemplation is an obscure but higher knowledge that God gives to the saint through their mutual love.

In infused contemplation the soul neither reflects nor reasons. It is simply silent. God and the soul gaze at each other, and in this quiet prayer the soul learns the "deep things of God" (1 Cor 2:10). Therefore, it is not a vision because it sees "without seeing," nor is it ordinary human knowledge, for it knows "without knowing."[3] And yet, it is precisely in this transluminous obscurity that the soul learns the things that God hides from the learned and reveals to the simple (cf. Mt 11:25).

---

[2] Saint John of the Cross, *The Dark Night,* Book II, Ch. 5, # 1, *op. cit.*, p. 97.

[3] Cf. *The Collected Works of Saint John of the Cross,* pp. 718-719.

Infused contemplation cannot be attained by one's efforts alone. It is not the same as the meditation of a *yogi* who deprives himself of every feeling, concept or imagination, to attain knowledge of Brahman. By the deliberate silencing of his passions and his mind, the *yogi* only discovers the wonderful reality of his *soul*. He finds *himself,* but does not find God. Now this is different from the infused contemplation of the saints, in which the soul finds God by losing itself or forgetting itself in Him.

Although infused contemplation cannot be acquired at will, the saints unanimously state that infused contemplation is *the natural summit of the interior life.* It is the perfection to which God ultimately leads a loving soul. As such, it is something that everyone may lawfully *seek.* For God does not merely want people to be saved. He also wants them to be perfect, even as He Himself is perfect (cf. Mt 5:48).

In holy contemplation the saint knows God in the act of loving and for the sake of love. Saint Albert the Great says that the contemplation of the philosophers is for the perfection of the one who contemplates and, therefore, terminates in the intellect. But the contemplation of the saints is for the love of God who is the object of contemplation. So, it does not stop in the intellect's knowledge, but passes into the heart by love.[4] In the saint's loving union with God, it acquires knowledge, not according to the human mode of concepts and reasoning, but by a kind of "contact" with the Divine. This "contact" with God is not yet the *beatific vision* of the Divine Essence enjoyed by the Blessed in Heaven, but it is superior to the knowledge of the most learned theologian. Through it the saint does not merely know things *about* God, but *experiences* God Himself. This is why Saint Bernard rightly says, "Reading seeks, meditation finds, contemplation *tastes.*"[5]

Contemplation and Action

Saint Thomas explains that certain things, while more excellent in themselves, may be surpassed by others in some respect. For example, a diamond may be more precious in itself than a piece of bread. However, there are cases when a piece of bread would be more valuable than a piece of diamond. So, Saint Thomas teaches that contemplation, considered in itself, is superior to action. However, because of the needs of the present life, we may regard the mixed life — the life of contemplation and action — as being the better state of

---

[4] *De Adhaerendo Deo,* Ch. IX.

[5] Saint Bernard, *Scala Claustralium.*

life for man.[6] In the present life in which one ought to help his neighbors attain salvation, a mixed life of prayer and action is at least more common, if not necessarily better than, a life of pure contemplation.

Considered in itself, the purely contemplative life is more excellent than the mixed life. Saint John of the Cross explains:

> It should be noted that until the soul reaches this state of union of love, she should practice love in both the active and contemplative life. Yet once she arrives, she should not become involved in other works and exterior exercises that might be of the slightest hindrance to the service of God. For a little of this pure love is more precious to God and the soul more beneficial to the Church, even though it seems one is doing nothing, than all these other works put together.[7]

Our Lord also tells Martha not to be troubled with many things because only one thing is necessary: *to love* (Lk 10:42). To dedicate oneself to the love and contemplation of God is to choose the better part.

---

[6] See Saint Thomas Aquinas, *Summa Theologiae*, II-II, q. 182, art. 1.

[7] Saint John of the Cross, *The Spiritual Canticle*, Stanza 29, # 2. See Kieran Kavanaugh's and Otilio Rodriguez's translation in *The Collected Works of St. John of the Cross* (Washington, DC: ICS Publications, 1973 paperback edition), p. 523.

Now we are ready to answer the criticism sometimes made by rationalists against the contemplative life. These rationalists want the contemplative to spend little time in prayer. They want him to go out into the world, and to work toward the elimination of misery and suffering. They condemn those who devote their time exclusively to prayer, and who apparently remain unmoved at the sight of widespread ignorance and poverty.

The true contemplative offers himself as a holocaust to hold the arm of God's justice, and yet the critics complain that he is unmoved! Thomas Merton reminds us not to confuse *insensitivity* with *detachment*. "The contemplative," he writes, "must certainly be detached, but he can never allow himself to become insensible to true human values, whether in society, in other men, or in himself."[8] The criticism of the rationalists contains a fundamental error. It mistakes the detachment of the contemplative person for the insensitivity of unconcerned souls. True contemplatives are not insensitive. They spend their time in silence and prayer, but their silent martyrdom is precious to the world. But the noisy critics would rather see them differently. They want the contemplatives to help the needy or fight an oppressor. They forget that hu-

---

8 Thomas Merton, *New Seeds of Contemplation* (New York: New Directions Books, 1972), Ch. 3, p. 20.

manitarianism is not necessarily charity. Often, they take pride in their speeches and their open fight against injustice. Yet, they in the world are ominously silent about the persecution of truth and the exaltation of vice. They want the contemplative to break his silence, forgetting that even in the human body the most vital functions — such as digestion, respiration, or the circulation of the blood — are realized in silence. The late Bishop Fulton Sheen once said, "It is the silent pool that reflects the stars."

A good contemplative is a friend of God. Although apparently he is doing nothing, the friendship he holds with God is more beneficial to the world than many external works that proceed from lesser charity. When a man loves a woman, he feels a high regard for everything that pertains to her. He is sympathetic to her friends and relatives, and shows an interest in her activities and her job. He normally prefers to spend time in her home, however humble it may be. For him, his beloved's home is not the same as any other house because the woman that he loves lives there. This is true of all lovers. It is equally true of God. If there is but one person whom God regards as His friend, then God will have a regard and sympathy for everything that pertains to him. Even the whole planet earth would be worth preserving for his sake. This is exactly how the contemplative benefits the world. Our world may be full of wickedness, but God tends to overlook the world's failings if He finds in it but one loving soul. Dom Marmion writes, "One might at times say that for such a soul God forgets the rest of the universe."[9]

In the Holy Scriptures we read how Abraham interceded to God for Sodom and Gomorrah. The Lord promised that He would spare the two cities if He could find but ten good men there (Gn 18:16-33). Of course, we read later that Sodom and Gomorrah were destroyed, implying that God did not find the ten good men that Abraham bargained for. In his private revelations to some mystics, however, God tells us that in the present world, it is not even necessary to find ten good men. He is willing to save the whole world for the sake of a *single* soul. For instance, our Lord said to Sor Bernarda Ezpelosin on June 16, 1882: "Yes, a generous soul giving itself wholly to me in sacrifice, is sufficient not only to sanctify one household, but also to save a nation and even the entire world."[10] To Venerable Ana Maria de la Concepción He said, "And I regard the city where you are with much consideration for your sake; for your love holds the arm of my justice bound and in your soul I find

---

[9] Dom Marmion, *Christ, The Ideal of a Monk*, Ch. 1.

[10] Sor Bernarda Ezpelosin, *Life*, p. 222.

rest from the evil treatment they give me in the world."[11]

In one sense, the mystic is like a living ciborium where Jesus dwells. But in another sense, the mystic is like a living *sacrament* itself, spreading God's goodness to its surroundings. He is, as it were, the point of contact between heaven and earth, the gate through which heavenly favors descend to the world. This is how the mystic benefits the world. God's mercy, indeed, can pardon, but only His love can renew the world. It is through the mystics, the living sacraments of God's love, that the Holy Spirit shall "renew the face of the earth" (Ps 103:30).

The Christian Apostolate

Saint Augustine says that God is so powerful that He can draw good even out of evil.[12] Correspondingly, the devil is so wicked that he can draw evil even out of good. The love of neighbor is a good thing in itself. But in his craftiness the devil manages to persuade many priests and religious to abandon the contemplative life "for the love of

---

[11] Ven. Ana Maria de la Concepción, *Life,* p. 31.

[12] Saint Augustine, *The Enchiridion on Faith, Hope and Love* (South Bend, IN: Regnery/Gateway, Inc., 1961), Ch. XI, p. 11.

neighbor." What a subtle way of dissipating the spiritual life in the Church!

It is true that our love for God is manifested by the love that we have for our neighbor. However, it is equally true that the love of neighbor is best accomplished through the friendship that we have with God. There is no better way of helping our neighbor than to intercede for them at the summit of mystical union. This is why Saint John of the Cross writes again:

> Let those, then, who are singularly active, who think they can win the world with their preaching and exterior works, observe here that they would profit the Church and please God much more, not to mention the good example they would give, were they to spend at least half of this time with God in prayer, even though they may not have reached a prayer as sublime as this.[13]

Besides, preaching and all other exterior works obtain their efficacy from contemplation. The trouble today is that many preachers have neglected to nourish their interior life with prayer. So, they are unable to quicken the life of others. "How

---

[13] Saint John of the Cross, *The Spiritual Canticle,* Stanza 29, # 3. See Kieran Kavanaugh's and Otilio Rodriguez's translation in *The Collected Works of St. John of the Cross* (Washington, DC: ICS Publications, 1973 paperback edition), p. 524.

is it," Saint Teresa asks, "that there are not many who are led by sermons to forsake open sin? Do you know what I think? That it is because preachers have too much worldly wisdom. They are not like the Apostles, flinging it all aside and catching fire with love for God; and so their flame gives little heat."[14] Therefore, the first task of any Christian worker or preacher is to keep God's love burning in his heart. The aim is not so much to illumine as to give off heat. Heat inflames the heart, and when people's hearts are afire, they will have their own light.

The Holy Scriptures remind us that where reflection is lacking, zeal is no good (Pr 19:2). Therefore, Vatican II admonished those who are dedicated to a life of contemplation to hold fast to their vocation no matter how pressing the needs of the apostolate may be.[15] Contemplation is the *fons et origo,* the wellspring of an effective Christian apostolate.

So, let us be clear about this. Contemplation is not ordered to action as a *means* to an end, but as an eminent *cause* to an inferior effect.[16] Contemplation is not the means to a fruitful apostolate. It

---

[14] Saint Teresa of Jesus, *The Autobiography of Saint Teresa of Jesus, op. cit.*, Ch. XVI, p. 167.

[15] Vatican II, *Decree on the Appropriate Renewal of the Religious Life,* #7.

[16] Reginald Garrigou-Lagrange, *The Three Ages of the Interior Life, op. cit.*, Vol. II, Ch. 48, p. 42.

is rather the *first cause* and the *end* of apostolic action. One does not contemplate to preach or to work. Rather, one preaches and works to bring others *to contemplation!*[17]

Therefore, preaching and other external works are more effective and beneficial to the Church when they overflow *from* the fullness of one's contemplation. It is not the other way around. Those who speak almost exclusively of activity *as if* activity *is identical to,* or *can replace,* contemplation, erroneously turn the Christian apostolate upside down. Of course, contemplation *can* be carried out in the midst of worldly activity. However, a contemplation-in-action, or a "noisy contemplation" such as that described by William Callahan,[18] can only be authentic if it springs from a silent contemplation originating from the depths of the soul. To speak of a masked contemplation in a very exclusive sense, *as if* contemplation can *arise* entirely from social action, is to forget that our active Lord also had to spend forty days in the desert before starting his public life. Those who think and speak *as if* social activity can be a *substitute* for

---

[17] Hence, the motto of the Dominicans: *Contemplari et contemplata aliis tradere.*

[18] William R. Callahan, SJ, "Noisy Contemplation," *The Wind is Rising, Prayer for Active People,* ed. by William R. Callahan, SJ and Francine Cardman (Mt. Rainer, MD: Quixote Center, 1978).

prayer and contemplation, forget that our Lord often had to withdraw from the crowd to pray. Prayer, fasting and the purification of the soul are the means to contemplation, which is the true source of the Christian apostolate. Experience shows that lovers of activity who neglect to temper their souls in prayer and contemplation, are exposed to deplorable falls and do not produce much fruit. As Saint Teresa said, all is smoke and noise.

The action that proceeds from the fullness of contemplation does not always consist in preaching and other external works of mercy. Sometimes, as we learn from the lives of so many saints, it also consists in *reparatory acts* for the sins of humankind. Saint Francis of Assisi was in this state for two years. Practically all saints, including the Little Flower of Lisieux, endured enormous sufferings in reparation not merely for their personal sins, but also for the sins of the rest of the world.[19]

People who think that contemplative people are merely wasting their energies, ought to remember this. If people are being saved, it is because there are in the world "victim souls" who suffer and

---

[19] Saint Thérèse narrates the "reparatory night" of her soul in her autobiography, *The Story of a Soul,* Ch. 9. Saint Catherine of Bologna endured the passive nights for 5 years; Blessed Henry Suso for 10 years; Saint Clara of Montefalco for 15 years, and Saint Teresa of Avila for 18 years!

pray for them. So, what the world needs today is not merely zealous apostles, or eloquent preachers, or efficient liberators. What the world needs above all is praying apostles, contemplative preachers, and more saints.

CHAPTER 5

MYSTICAL EXPERIENCES

Mystical Phenomena

In the past people regarded mysticism and its associated phenomena with much skepticism. This was the situation until the prominent American psychologist, William James (1842-1910), recognized the existence of genuine *mystical states of consciousness* in some people.[1] Following his leadership, scholars today no longer dismiss the mystical experiences of spiritual people as downright unreal. However, a few comments must be made about the views that William James expressed in his book, *The Varieties of Religious Experience*.

William James reported several cases of people who had experienced brief moments of "mystical consciousness." In these experiences, the witnesses said that they felt an extraordinary sense of "oneness" with the Absolute. Apparently, however, these experiences were not entirely supernatural because James said that they could be induced by drugs, such as nitrous oxide, ether or chloroform. James also noted that mysticism as a religious experience is not peculiar to the Christian religion. There are mystics also among Buddhists, Hindus and Muslims. Finally, he concluded that mystical

---

[1] William James, *The Varieties of Religious Experience* (New York: The Modern Library, 1902), Lectures XVI and XVII.

experiences do not necessarily support belief in an infinite God. "The only thing that it unequivocally testifies to is that we can experience union with *something* larger than ourselves and in that union find our greatest peace."[2]

First, I think that true mystical experiences are not identical to the "mystical states" cited by William James. Christian saints are unanimous in their testimony that God Himself was responsible for their mystical experiences, and that they could not by their efforts alone cause them. So, the drug-induced experiences mentioned by William James cannot be true mystical experiences, if "mystical" means an experience *of,* and *from,* God. Perhaps the intoxication by nitrous oxide calls into play the same physiological functions that are usually involved in genuine mystical phenomena. If this is so, then the mental state of the recipient will have the material semblance of a mystical state. But in the absence of a divine element and origin, this state cannot be anything more than an abnormal state of consciousness.

Also, after coming from their mystical prayers, the saints claimed that they had a *subjective certitude* that it was God Himself whom they beheld, though obscurely, in the depths of their

---

[2] William James, *The Varieties of Religious Experience,* Postscript, p. 515.

souls. It was not just "something larger than ourselves." In contrast, James' "mystics" make no
claims of having encountered God (except when
they *philosophize* and equate all of reality with God
Himself). Their testimonies only indicate a sudden,
powerful, and often joyful *intuition* of the unity of
all beings. Now, this intuition itself may be a gift
of God. But it is *not* an intellectual vision of God.
Much less is it the kind of "divine union" described
by the saints. It is more like the sudden intimations
of *beauty* that naturally come to poets and artists
through their "communion with nature."

The mystical states experienced by members
of Eastern religions is similar. The Eastern mystic
perceives the Self within the depths of his soul. By
deliberately obliterating all ideas and thoughts from
his consciousness, a *yogi,* for example, can get a
glimpse of that wonderful reality deep within himself. But there is nothing supernatural about this.
It is no more than a penetrating insight, attained
without and *beyond* reasoning, of the interior of the
soul. Those who see their souls in this manner think
that they have seen God. This is not surprising, for
the soul is made in the image and likeness of God
(Gn 1:26).

However, the infused contemplation of the
saints is altogether different. To show the difference, let me first present the "mystical theology"
contained, for instance, in the *Bhagavad Gita.*

Later Hindu philosophers make a distinction between Atman, Saguna Brahman and Nirguna Brahman. The term "Atman" denotes God as immanent in man. "Saguna Brahman" denotes God as immanent in the universe. And "Nirguna Brahman" denotes God as transcending both the universe and man. However, they also say that the true Self that is within us (Atman) *is* Brahman. The trouble is that the identification of the world and ourselves with the "self that is within all beings" is not readily apparent. The things that we perceive, including ourselves, are perishable, whereas Brahman is unchanging and imperishable.[3] Therefore, according to this philosophy, the world of our perceptions cannot be the real Brahman, but only the illusion or manifestation of Brahman. This illusion is due to *maya,* or the capability of Brahman to hide himself. Thus, He says: "I am not manifest to all, being veiled by My mysterious power (Yoga-maya). This ignorant world does not know Me, the unborn and immutable."[4]

---

[3] Arguna said: "You are the imperishable, the Supreme, the thing to be known, You are the supreme resting place of this universe, You are the undecaying and the preserver of the eternal religion; I regard you as the primeval Being." — *Bhagavad Gita,* Ch. XI, verse 18. Tr. by Swami Vireswarananda in *Srimad-Bhagavad-Gita,* (Mylapore, Madras-4: Sri Ramakrishna Math, 1948), p. 323.

[4] *Bhagavad Gita,* Chapter VII, Verse 25, *op. cit.*, p. 229.

The aim of every person should therefore be to attain the true Self that is hidden behind his illusory self. He who fails to attain his true Self will remain in this illusory world. After death his Self will again assume another form. This means that he will be born again perhaps as another man, a plant or a swine (reincarnation). To escape this cycle, a person must earnestly seek to attain his true Self. He can achieve this by striving for absolute immobility, by quieting his senses, his mind and all his desires. When he succeeds, he will see his true Self, and through itself, all things. For the true Self (Atman) is Brahman, the universal form of all things. In the contemplation of the universal form the *Yogi* will find immortality and supreme happiness. Thus, we read in the *Bhagavad Gita*:

> The Blessed Lord said:
> Ch. V, verse 26: "Sages who are free from passion and anger, who have controlled their mind, and who have realized the Self, attain absorption in Brahman here and hereafter."
> Ch. VI, verse 4: "When one habitually renounces all desires and is no more attached either to sense-objects or to actions, then one is said to have attained to Yoga."
> Ch. VI, verse 28: "The Yogi entirely free from taint, constantly controlling the mind thus, attains easily the infinite bliss of union with Brahman."

Ch. VI, verse 29: "The man whose mind is absorbed through Yoga and who sees the same (Brahman) everywhere, sees the Self in all beings and all beings in the Self."
Ch. XIII, verse 12: "I shall tell you that which has to be known, knowing which one attains immortality; it is the beginningless, supreme Brahman, which is said to be neither being nor non-being."[5]

Some writers find in Yoga spirituality a remarkable similarity with the mysticism of the saints. They claim that the Yoga experience is the common ground where all religions meet. However, I am not so quick to water down Christianity in this fashion. A moment's reflection will show that true mystical experience is distinct from, and irreducible to, the "peak experiences" of a Yoga practitioner.

First, true mysticism cannot be attained simply by denuding one's self of all ideas, passions and feelings. To do this is to enter into an artificial state of being one with oneself, rather than of being one with a transcendent God. Mystical union requires the super-elevation of human nature by grace for an act of *friendship* with God. So, it does not consist in silencing the passions, but in harmonizing them toward the love of God.

---

[5] *Ibid.*

Second, since intimacy and friendship with a transcendent God belongs to the supernatural order, mystical union in the Christian religion is not something that a person can attain by his personal efforts alone. To help him come to this exalted state, God normally sends the frightful "nights of the soul" described by Saint John of the Cross. Now, the similarity of this purification with Hindu asceticism is nothing but superficial. It is true that the Hindu mystic also avoids overeating and other bodily excesses. He renounces all such actions and relinquishes their effects. But the intent of Hindu asceticism is to free oneself from the cosmic illusions of *maya* and the suffering that results from the recurring cycle of death and rebirth. In contrast, the "nights of the soul" aim to purify the heart from *sin* and from attachment to anything that separates a person from God. The purification of the saints aims to free the aspirant from *moral,* not merely *physical,* evil. This cannot be said of Hindu mysticism. Since in Hindu philosophy the Self within us is the God (Brahman) without, there cannot be a true moral obligation in Hindu ethics. Moral obligation implies the existence of a Lawgiver distinct from the subject. Therefore, the notion of evil in Hindu ethics is merely one of bodily pain, rather than a moral offence against a distinct and transcendent Creator.

I do not deny that there may be cases of authentic mystical experience outside Christianity. Too often, however, as in Catholic experience itself, commercial interests and an undue love of the spectacular creep in to destroy whatever is good in these cults. I believe that if cases of genuine mystical experience are found in other religions, they arise by a spiritual affinity with the life of Christ Himself. For Christ is the principle of all grace as He is the Redeemer of humankind (Rm 5:19). The Catholic Church has members other than baptized Catholics. She regards as her "invisible" members those who, though belonging to other religions through no fault of their own, earnestly seek and love God as their Lord and Savior. God makes friends everywhere. So, it is possible that God also raises people of other faiths to the heights of contemplative prayer.

Ordinary Supernatural Phenomena

Let me now discuss the various phenomena that sometimes accompany the prayers of the saints. These phenomena are not absolutely necessary for contemplation, but they have helped some people.

The most common of these phenomena is *ecstasy*. This happens when a person is so absorbed in prayer that, by a special favor from the Lord, he perceives in prayer the infinite majesty of God Himself. The phenomenon consists in a certain suspension of the exterior senses, manifested by the lack of sensation and a lowering of body temperature. Saint Teresa of Avila describes this, saying: "In these raptures the soul seems no longer to animate the body, and thus the natural heat of the body is felt to be very sensibly diminished: it gradually becomes colder, though conscious of the greatest sweetness and delight."[6]

Occasionally the suspension of the senses is incomplete and allows the ecstatic to do other things. For example, Saint Catherine of Siena dictated her *Dialogue* while in ecstasy. The Franciscan sister, Sor Beatriz de la Concepción, served in the refectory while in ecstasy. Complete ecstasy ordinarily lasts for some minutes only. However, there are complete ecstasies that have lasted for days. For example, Saint Ignatius was in ecstasy for 8 days. Saint Magdalen of Pazzi for 40 days! It all depends on God.

Some critics of mysticism have tried to discredit ecstasy by regarding it as a form of hysteria. Yet there is a big difference between the genuine ecstatic and the neuropathic or hysterical person. The mystic manifests great peace of soul and shows

---

[6] Saint Teresa of Jesus, *The Autobiography of Saint Teresa of Jesus, op. cit.*, Ch. XX, p. 190.

no sign of abnormal emotionalism. Instead of getting weak, the ecstatic physically gains new strength. The effects on the spiritual plane are also different. The mystic exhibits exemplary obedience, heroic courage, great virtue, and a superior knowledge of heavenly things.

Another very common phenomenon among the saints is the *transverberation* or *wound of love.* This is a very painful experience of love that happens when the saint desires so much to be united with God and yet learns that death is still far away. Experiences such as this inspired the following lines from the poetry of Saint John of the Cross:

> This life that I live
> Is no life at all,
> And so I die continually
> Until I live with You;
> Hear me, my God:
> I do not desire this life,
> I am dying because I do not die.[7]

In its ardent longing for the Beloved, the saint experiences a terrible pain — spiritual, yes, but

---

[7] Saint John of the Cross, "Stanzas of the Soul that Suffers with Longing to See God," Stanza #2. Tr. by Kieran Kavanaugh, OCD and Otilio Rodriguez, OCD in *The Collected Works of St. John of the Cross* (Washington, DC: ICS Publications, 1973 paperback edition), p. 720. Saint Teresa of Jesus wrote a similar poem, "Vivo sin vivir en mí…" See *The Complete Works of Saint Teresa,* tr. by E. Allison Peers (Sheed and Ward, 1957), Volume III, pp. 277-279.

touching the most profound depths of the soul. Saint Teresa of Avila, who also experienced this, describes it thus:

> While the soul is in this condition, and interiorly burning, it often happens that a mere fleeting thought of some kind (there is no way of telling whence it comes, or how) or some remark which the soul hears about death's long tarrying, deals it, as it were, a blow, or, as one might say, wounds it with an arrow of fire.[8]

Yet the pain is sweet and the soul desires it, clearly showing that it is from God. The devil cannot effect such an experience in the soul since it cannot combine pain with tranquility.

There are other supernatural phenomena that take place in souls that are still under trial. These are the frightful "nights of the soul" spoken of by Saint John of the Cross.

Note that ecstasy, the wound of love, and the dark nights are *supernatural* phenomena. Therefore, they are beyond our powers to produce. And yet, these phenomena are not in any way "extraordinary" in the strict sense of the word. For they are found in practically all mystics. Ecstasy is an ordinary phenomenon to a person who is deeply ab-

---

[8] Saint Teresa of Jesus, *The Interior Castle,* Sixth Mansion, Chapter 11, *op. cit.*, p. 197.

sorbed in contemplation. The spiritual wounds are also ordinary to one who is deeply in love with a God whom he could not fully see. Therefore, these phenomena must be distinguished from those charismatic gifts that are truly extraordinary; namely, visions, locutions, levitation, *etc.* These last-mentioned phenomena are also supernatural, but they are special favors that God grants, not merely for the benefit of the recipient, but for the good of the Church at large.

It is important to keep this distinction between the "ordinary" and the "extraordinary" phenomena clear in our minds. The so-called transluminous but obscure knowledge learned in secret while the soul is in the state of contemplation, is "ordinary" and may legitimately be desired. For it is the normal fruit of contemplative prayer. But the knowledge of a future free event, seen in an imaginary vision, is strictly "extraordinary." And God grants this gift not merely for the good of the individual, but for the improvement of the whole Church. The desire for such and similar supernatural favors is not *per se* sinful, if God's glory and the progress of the soul to virtue are earnestly sought. However, the desire for extraordinary gifts is not without its dangers, since vanity and pride can creep in even in the desire for something good.

Extraordinary Supernatural Phenomena

The extraordinary phenomena associated with mysticism are not many, and I will describe them only briefly since they are accidental to mysticism as such. Being purely charismatic, these phenomena should not, according to many writers, be desired. Therefore, they say, it would be wrong to wish to see a vision, or to wish to prophesy or to perform miracles. Strictly, however, these extraordinary gifts are not evil in themselves. They are profitable in many cases, not only to the faithful, but also to the recipients of such graces. That they should not be desired at all, is not true *per se*. If spiritual masters have discouraged many a pious soul from desiring these charismatic gifts, it was only to avoid the hidden presumption, vanity, or curiosity that often mingle with such desires. But these extraordinary favors coming from the Lord are certainly good in themselves, and they cannot be anything but desirable.[9] Saint Paul tells the Thessalonians, "Do not stifle the spirit or despise prophecies" (1 Th 5:19-20). He says the same to the Corinthians: "Therefore, brethren, set your hearts on prophecy, but do not forbid speaking in tongues" (1 Cor 14:39). However, he adds this

---

[9] See John G. Arintero, *The Mystical Evolution, op. cit.*, Vol. II, Part II, Ch. VII, Footnote 26, pp. 310-311.

important admonition, "But let everything be done in a proper and orderly fashion" (1 Cor 14:40). Even the Apostle, therefore, while telling us to be ambitious with regard to these extraordinary gifts, has not neglected to warn us of their dangers. Also, recall that it was the same Apostle who taught us that charity is better than all extraordinary graces: "But strive for the greatest gifts. And I will show you an even better way" (1 Cor 12:31).

The following are the most common extraordinary graces:

Rapture. This is essentially the same as ecstasy, but different only in origin. Ecstasy is felt sweetly by a person that is ardently loving God in prayer and contemplation. In contrast, rapture comes abruptly to a person to bring him to holy contemplation. Unlike ecstasy, therefore, rapture *precedes* rather than follows contemplation. This is why Saint Thomas makes this comment: "Ecstasy means simply a going out of oneself by being placed outside one's proper order; while rapture denotes a certain violence in addition."[10] The phenomenon of rapture is irresistible, God Himself being its Author. We play no part in causing it. It comes unexpectedly and permeates the whole person in a

---

[10] Saint Thomas Aquinas, *Summa Theologiae*, Part II-II, q. 175, art. 2, Reply to Obj. 1., *op. cit.*, Vol. 2, p. 1914.

moment. It happens anytime and anywhere God wills to grant such a favor, even in a public place, and even when the recipient is not praying. At its height, this may ravish the recipient so that he neither sees, nor hears, nor feels. And yet, he does not lose his consciousness. No harm comes to the body. Rather, it experiences pleasant sensations. After the rapture the body may not be able to move even for a long time. Afterwards, if it is a true rapture, the recipient is no longer content to serve God in small things, although he may still serve Him only in a little way. Rapture causes a great desire in the recipient to serve God in greater things.

Transport. This phenomenon often accompanies a violent rapture. It has sometimes been called "flight of the spirit." It happens when a person, although in full possession of his senses, is suddenly rapt away with such violence that the body is transported, too. Levitation, or the lifting up of the body from the ground, is an instance of this transport. In this case, the body becomes light, so light that it could be blown and carried by the wind. Saint Teresa of Jesus testifies that one does not lose consciousness during levitation.[11] Saint Catherine de Ricci frequently walked in procession

---

[11] Saint Teresa of Jesus, *The Autobiography of Saint Teresa of Jesus, op. cit.*, Ch. XX, p. 196.

with other nuns without touching the ground. The case of Saint Agnes the Virgin exhibits a contrary effect. When dragged by her persecutors, her body became mysteriously fixed on the ground!

Bilocation. This is an astounding phenomenon in which the body is not merely transported to a distant place, but is also duplicated. Cases of bilocation were observed in the lives of Saint Nicholas of Myra, Saint Anthony of Padua, Saint Francis Xavier and others. People saw them in places far from where their bodies were.

Stigmata. This consists in a person's acquiring in his or her body a duplication of the wounds of Christ. The first recorded case was that of Saint Francis of Assisi, who reproduced in his body the wounds of Christ. Many, but not all, of the mystics were stigmatists. Teresa Neumann and Padre Pio are very recent cases. Could a genuine stigmata be caused by suggestion or autosuggestion? The answer is a frank "No!" The stigmata have many peculiar characteristics that could not be explained by science. For one thing, the stigmata cannot be cured. They form and heal by themselves, without the aid of anything short of supernatural power. The wounds do not smell; sometimes, they even emit a fragrant odor. Often, the wounds, as well as the bleeding, occur periodically according to the mysteries of the liturgical year, being more frequent on the Fridays of Lent. The abundant flow of blood is difficult to explain also, since the wounds are located far from large arteries. Also, when the patient is lying on his back, the blood flows from the wound in his feet *upward,* contrary to the direction of gravity. This is because the phenomenon attempts to reproduce the flow of blood on the feet of our Lord as He hung on the cross. In the case of Saint Francis and Teresa Neumann the stigmata did not merely reproduce the blood and the wounds. They are even said to have reproduced the form of the nails that caused the wounds![12]

Divine Revelations. Although divine revelations have also been given in the form of intellectual visions, many private revelations are in the form of sensible *visions* or apparitions. The recipient sees a saint or an event either by the imagination (while awake or during sleep) or by the bodily eyes. Often the apparition is accompanied by the hearing of sensible words, such as when the recipient is in conversation with a saint, the Blessed Virgin, or Jesus Christ. The words, which are often audible but to the recipient only, are known as *locutions.* Many spiritual writers discourage the faithful from desiring private revelations of this kind

---

[12] Charles M. Carty, *The Stigmata and Modern Science* (Rockford, IL: TAN Books, 1974).

because these can easily be produced also by the devil.[13] According to Saint Paul, Satan often goes about disguised as an angel of light (2 Cor 11:14). To carry out his wicked plans, the devil could appear and talk to a human person while pretending to be an angel or a saint. Therefore, there is no absolute guarantee that an apparition is of divine origin, even if it is simultaneously witnessed by two or more people. The Church exercises great caution in recognizing the authenticity of apparitions and private revelations. When the Church approves them, She merely affirms that they contain nothing that is opposed to the Bible or to Church teachings. For this reason, they may be revealed to others for their *pious belief* and reflection, but not necessarily for their strict adherence or compliance. Private revelations are not part of the Catholic faith. So, even when they carry ecclesiastical approval, they are *not* strictly infallible. Still, when a person receives these visions or locutions from the Lord, he should, like Joan of Arc, believe them firmly, especially if they are accompanied by other signs

---

[13] Visions and apparitions are not necessary for sanctity. And, because of the pride and vanity that often accompany the desire for them, some spiritual writers regard such desires to be *at least* a venial sin. Cf. Saint John of the Cross, *The Ascent of Mount Carmel,* Book II, Ch. 21, in Kieran Kavanaugh, OCD and Otilio Rodriguez's translation: *The Collected Works of St. John of the Cross* (Washington, DC: ICS Publications, 1973 paperback edition), p. 174.

that indicate the divine origin of such apparitions.

Wonders. These include all other phenomena not mentioned above. For example, some saints obtained privileges similar to those given to our first parents in the state of innocence. Some, such as Saint Martin de Porres, recover primitive dominion over wild beasts and over nature. Others, like Saint Catherine of Siena, could spend long periods without food or drink save the Holy Eucharist. Saint Catherine was in this state for 12 years! More remarkable still was Saint Nicholas of Flüe, who took no food for 20 years, a fact that was rigorously established even during his lifetime. There were others still who spent long periods without sleep. On record was Saint Ludwina, whose sleep over 35 years was equivalent to only one full night. Then there are also some saints whose bodies radiated light or perfume (the luminous and fragrant *effluvia*). These things are certainly wonderful, for they give us even now some notion of what our future, glorified bodies will be like.

CHAPTER 6

THE SECRET OF THE SAINTS

Jesus Wants Saints, Not Just Good People

Due to the incorrect association of "extraordinary graces" with sanctity, many people get the impression that the desire for sanctity is vain. They think that genuine mysticism is only for a privileged few. This view leads to a sad consequence: *mediocrity* in the spiritual life. Some spiritual guides no longer talk even of ordinary supernatural phenomena anymore, and they fail to encourage others from aspiring for the "infused contemplation" of the saints. They rather emphasize the practice of "acquired contemplation" through meditation and common prayers. Because of this, many fervent souls, whose piety and ability give excellent promise of a perfect life, are held back from advancing along the way of perfection. They feed on devotional and spiritual books languishing in mediocrity and wanting in depth. These books tend sometimes to retard rather than accelerate the progress of the person toward an heroic life of holiness.

Yet, spirituality is not dead in the present world, nor have people ceased to relish the things that are spiritual. But because of the superficiality that they find in the spiritual life of so many Christians, a number of them are turning toward the spurious mysticism of the New Age cults rather than to the authentic mysticism of the saints. I have great compassion for these people. To borrow a metaphor from Saint Mark, "they are like sheep without a shepherd" (Mk 6:34).

We can dispel this prejudice against sanctity and infused contemplation if we reflect that Christ came into the world to produce not just good people, but saints. He said, "I have come that you may have life, and *may have it more abundantly*" (Jn 10:10). The precept to love God admits no limit: "You shall love the Lord your God *with all your heart, and with all your soul, and with all your strength*" (Dt 6:5). God detests mediocrity: "And so, because you are lukewarm, and neither hot nor cold, I will vomit you out of my mouth" (Rv 3:16).

"Be therefore perfect, as your heavenly Father is perfect" (Mt 5:48), says our Lord. Now, what does this mean if not that the call to perfection is not reserved for a privileged few, but is addressed to everyone? Indeed, not all are called to become priests. Not all need to make the religious vows or live in religious congregations. But all are invited to become *saints.*

But many people hesitate to answer this invitation. They feel that they cannot perform miracles and wonders as the saints did. They feel that they cannot suffer as the martyrs did. However, as Saint Thérèse of Lisieux teaches, one can also be a saint in a "little way." One does not have to perform miracles. It is enough to offer every little work, every little glance, and every little word spoken, to God. One can be a saint just by being extraordinarily faithful to one's ordinary duties in life. He who lives by this teaching may be certain that no matter how little he may appear to himself, he also will be able in the final moment to suffer even martyrdom. "He who is faithful in very small matters, is faithful also in those which are greater" (Lk 16:10).

This is why many spiritual writers speak highly of the "little way" of Saint Thérèse. It is important, though, not to have any illusions about this. As I will show next, even the "little way" of Saint Thérèse is not a superficial way. It is "ordinary" only because it does not require the accompaniment of miracles and other extraordinary graces. It does not mean that it excludes infused contemplation and the other ordinary supernatural phenomena associated with it.

The Little Way of Spiritual Childhood

In her life and writings Saint Thérèse of Lisieux, the most recent Doctor of the Church, taught us a sure and simple way to sanctity. According to her, one does not have to perform miracles or suffer bloody persecutions to become a saint. It is enough to love God and to trust Him, as a child loves and trusts its father. This is her authentic teaching. It is known in spiritual literature as "The Little Way of Spiritual Childhood."

The "little way" is not a new teaching. Nor did Saint Thérèse invent it. It is found in the Gospels: "Amen I say to you, unless you be converted, and become as little children, you shall not enter the kingdom of heaven" (Mt 18:3). Saint Paul, too, was extolling spiritual childhood when he said, "God chose the foolish of the world to shame those who are wise, the weak of the world to shame the strong" (1 Cor 1:27).

But what does it mean to be a spiritual child? We can find the answer to this question if we consider some of the characteristics of children. First, children are *simple*. They possess no duplicity of character. They do not pretend to be what they are not. They show no hypocrisy. They talk and behave according to what they have in their heart.

Second, children are *aware of their weakness*. This awareness is the source of their humility. Because of it, children recognize the power of their father. As Fulton Sheen noted, to every child his father is a giant. Yet, although children know their father to be mighty, they do not fear him. They love and trust him fully. This is the third characteristic of children. *They love, trust, and have confidence in their father.*

Of course, children have other characteristics, such as their attachment to food, toys and their unrestrained behavior. These are not necessarily bad, but unbecoming to the children of God. This is why spiritual childhood is not the same as natural childhood. Like Saint Paul (cf. 1 Cor 14:20), Saint Thérèse tells us to be a spiritual child, not a natural child; to be childlike, but not childish.

In recommending her secret of sanctity, Saint Thérèse admonishes us to be simple. The Holy Scriptures abound with passages that show how God praises simplicity and hates duplicity.[1] Also, Saint Thérèse tells us to recognize God's greatness in our littleness, and God's mercy in our weakness. She knows that out wretchedness is precisely what most attracts God to us.[2] Our frailty is irresistible to His Heart. Our weakness is His weakness.

So, Saint Thérèse's confidence in God was not due to her knowledge of her innocence, but to her knowledge of God's mercy and love. "It is not because I have been preserved from mortal sin that I fly to God with loving confidence. I know I should still have this confidence even if my conscience were burdened with every possible crime."[3]

---

[1] Wisdom 1:5; Hosea 10:2; Matthew 10:16; Colossians 3:22.

[2] Saint Thomas also said that God does not love us because we are good. Rather, we are good because God loves us. *Summa Theologiae,* Part I, q. 20, art. 2.

[3] Saint Thérèse of Lisieux, *The Story of a Soul, op. cit.*, Ch. 10, p. 149.

If we follow the little way of spiritual childhood, it would be unnecessary to work miracles and extraordinary deeds to attain the heights of sanctity. It is sufficient to love God and, for the sake of that love, to do ordinary things extraordinarily well. What a relief this is for most of us! Like Saint Thérèse, we feel that we cannot perform miracles and all the heavy mortifications practiced by the saints. Thérèse herself wished that she could be as great a saint as the martyrs were. She wanted to be flayed like Saint Bartholomew, or flung into burning oil like Saint John. But like so many of us, she realized that the "great way" was not for her. She offered us instead her "little way," the way of spiritual childhood:

> Jesus has shown me the only path which leads to this divine furnace of love. It is the complete abandonment of a baby sleeping without fear in its father's arms.... Charity gave me the key to *my vocation.* I realized that if the Church was a body made up of different members, she would not be without the greatest and most essential of them all.... At last I have found my vocation. My vocation is love! I have found my place in the bosom of the Church and it is You, Lord, who have given it to me. In the heart of the Church, who is my Mother, *I will be love....* Great deeds are forbidden me, I cannot preach the Gospel nor shed my blood — but what does it

matter? My brothers toil instead of me and I, a little child, well, I keep close by the throne of God and I *love* for those who fight. Love proves itself by deeds, so how am I to show my love? Well, I will scatter flowers, perfuming the divine Throne with their fragrance, and I'll sweetly sing my hymn of love.[4]

Here, then, is the secret of the saints. To reach God, only one thing is necessary, and that is *to love God with all your heart*. This is the way of the saints, the "excellent way" indicated by Saint Paul. This is also the "little way" of Saint Thérèse. It is "little" because it requires the accomplishment of no miracle. I do not mean that it involves no supernatural phenomena at all. This cannot be, for grace of itself is *supernatural*. I do not mean that the "little way" is an easy way either. It is easy only to one who already loves perfectly. To most of us who are still learning to love, the path to sanctity requires rigorous discipline and much prayer. Sin and vice must still be crushed. The "old man" must still die. Therefore, even those who wish to follow the way of spiritual childhood need to go through the purifications indicated by the great masters of spirituality. Everybody still needs to be purified by the "nights of the soul" described by Saint John of the Cross. Saint

---

[4] *Op cit.,* Ch. 11, pp. 150-157.

Thérèse herself was not exempt from this.[5]

Therefore, those who tell us that mysticism today should have none of the affective prayers, purifications and supernatural experiences of the saints, might be missing the point. Don't we realize that what many people need today is depth and authenticity in their spiritual life? Don't we realize that many young people are turning toward the Eastern religions because they do not want a superficial Christianity anymore? They need *friendship* with a God that they can talk to "deep within," not an unreachable God "up there."

Doubtless, an overdose of mystical literature in the hands of indiscreet individuals can produce "instant mystics" and long-faced psychopaths. But this aberration is no excuse for penalizing those who are eagerly seeking God. To do so is similar to starve your children just because some thoughtless kids became sick from overeating. Mediocrity and a mysticism of the commonplace cannot be our sole end. Even the "little way" of Saint Thérèse should find its climax in the *infused contemplation* of the saints.

---

[5] See St. Thérèse's *The Story of a Soul,* Ch. 9, where she describes the dark tunnel that her soul had to go through.

Mysticism and the Rosary

There is one more secret that must be mentioned here, one that will make the road to sanctity a lot easier for many people. I am here referring to the path indicated by the Blessed Virgin Mary herself, the Mother of God and our Mother. In the first chapter of this book I spoke of the need to approach Jesus through Mary. Here I will speak of one particular prayer that Mary recommends above all others, and that is the daily recitation of her Most Holy Rosary.

Some experts on Christian spirituality might be surprised by this recommendation. They think that because the Rosary consists in *meditation* and the *verbal* recitation of the Our Father, the Hail Mary's and the Glory Be's, then it is a prayer that is fit only for beginners but not for the proficients. However, I maintain that the Holy Rosary is a prayer that is fit *even for the perfect!*

Let us not forget that the *contemplation* of the mysteries of our faith is the *soul* of the Rosary, and that many people have reached the summit of spiritual life in this manner. Saint Francis de Sales, Saint Ignatius, Saint Teresa, Saint Alphonsus Liguori, and so many other saints and mystics of the Church, openly manifested their devotion to the Most Holy Rosary. Even Queen Blanche of Castille and Saint

King Louis of France were ardent devotees of the Rosary.

The Holy Rosary can be prayed not only meditatively but also *affectively,* and it is in this manner that Mary leads the proficients and the perfect to pray it. The Rosary is a simple prayer, which is why some experts fail to see its wisdom and its power. The simplicity of this prayer eludes their bookish learning. Provided that the aspirant *seeks* God honestly and earnestly, then, even when he cannot meditate successfully, the verbal recitation itself of the Hail Mary's is most pleasing to our Mother. It constantly reminds her of that joyful event when the Archangel Gabriel announced to her that she was to be the Mother of God.

One may ask, are not the great spiritual writers unanimous in their affirmation that the most lofty prayers involve no meditation, words, or ideas? Do not the verbal recitation of the Rosary and its meditation block the ascent of a person to mystical union with God? Saint Louis Marie Grignion de Montfort (1673-1716), warns us that such is the great lie that the devil uses to stop people from praying the Rosary:

> I admit it is not always necessary to say them as vocal prayers and that interior prayer is, in a sense, more perfect than vocal. But believe me, it is really dangerous, not to say fatal, to give up saying the Rosary of your own accord under the

pretext of seeking a more perfect union with
God. Sometimes a soul that is proud in a subtle
way and who may have done everything that he
can do interiorly to rise to the sublime heights
of contemplation that the saints have reached
may be deluded by the noonday devil into giving up his former devotions which are good
enough for ordinary souls.[6]

So, he advises those who have not yet reached the
state of union to continue praying the Rosary.

But if you are still in the state of active contemplation or the usual prayer of quietude, of the
presence of God, affective prayer, you have even
less reason for giving up the Rosary. Far from
making you lose ground in mental prayer or
stunting your spiritual growth, it will be a wonderful help to you. You will find it a real Jacob's
ladder with fifteen rungs by which you will go
from virtue to virtue and from light to light.
Thus, without danger of being misled, you will
easily arrive at the fullness of the age of Jesus
Christ.[7]

And for those who have already made great
progress in prayer, he says:

---

[6] Saint Louis Marie Grignion de Montfort, *Secret of the Rosary*,
Twenty-Fifth Rose, as translated in *God Alone: The Collected Writings of St. Louis Marie de Montfort* (Bay Shore, NY: Montfort Publications, 1987), p. 190.

[7] *Ibid*, p. 191.

If you have already attained, by the grace of God, a high degree of prayer, keep up the practice of saying the holy Rosary if you wish to remain in that state and by it to grow in humility. For never will anyone who says his Rosary every day become a formal heretic or be led astray by the devil. This is a statement which I would sign with my blood.

On the other hand, if God in His infinite mercy draws you to himself as forcibly as he did some of the saints while saying the Rosary, make yourself passive in his hands and let yourself be drawn towards him. Let God work and pray in you and *let him say your Rosary in his way,* and that will be sufficient for the day.[8]

There you are. It is true that the great spiritual writers said that at the summit of mystical union, the saint converses with God without the need of so many words and ideas. But the great spiritual writers also said that in mystical union, God and the saint are one. During the night when the saint cannot meditate and yet recites the Rosary lovingly and patiently, it is the Holy Spirit Himself who says the Hail Mary through him. What a beautiful doctrine!

He who prays the Rosary will soon discover

---

[8] *Ibid.,* pp. 190-191. Italics added. See Rm 8:26, "...the Spirit also helps us in our weakness, for we don't know how to pray as we should; instead, the Spirit himself pleads for us with inexpressible groanings."

that the daily recitation of the Rosary is not easy. First, there is the problem of time. People today do not seem to have time to pray. However, as the new *Catechism of the Catholic Church* (#2710) says, one does not pray only when one has the time: "One makes time for the Lord." Second, it is not easy to meditate. Unlike other prayers, which consist of a variety of words and gestures, the constant repetition of the Our Father's and Hail Mary's of the Rosary tires the soul and makes one vulnerable to a lot of distractions. But it is precisely here, when the aspirant feels that he is no longer praying effectively, or when he feels that he is only paying lip service to Our Lady, that the Blessed Mother effectively gives her Son. Provided, therefore, that he seeks God honestly, and prays lovingly though blindly, he should never give up the Rosary.

It has often been said that when one cannot meditate, then one must be silent. This is true in general, but *not when one is praying the Rosary!* One does not need to stop the meditation of the mysteries deliberately just to seek a more perfect union with God. To do so would be to fall into the error of the Quietists. After all, as Saint Teresa testifies, one *cannot* truly resist God when He wishes to bring a person to contemplation.[9] If God wants to bring

---

[9] Cf. Saint Teresa of Avila, *The Interior Castle,* Fourth Mansion, Ch. III, p. 90. For this reason, even Saint Teresa does not think it nec-

a person to this state of prayer, the prayerful person will not be able to resist being silent even when he tries. He will be powerless and wholly *passive* as God brings Him to this state, and from this prayer into the Night of the Spirit that leads to mystical union. He will suffer enormously because of the seeming worthlessness of his prayers. However, his suffering is precious, for it is the suffering of one who loves.

So, let him who is having difficulty in meditating the mysteries of the Rosary simply *continue* this prayer and *not* abandon it. He is very close to the heart of God. As Saint Louis de Montfort says, it is the Holy Spirit Himself who prays through him. It is in suffering and in the obscurity of his mind that the Blessed Mother shall convert his "wordy" prayers into prayers of transforming union.

Of course, the Rosary is not the only way to pray. But the Blessed Mother has promised, and the Supreme Pontiffs agreed, that in the present world the holy Rosary is the instrument that will bring many human hearts into intimate union with Jesus.[10]

---

essary to abandon meditation of your own accord: "For in the Prayer of Recollection it is unnecessary to abandon meditation and the activities of the understanding." Further on, she warns those who abandon meditation and enter a make-believe prayer of quiet in this manner: "So they get it into their heads that it is *arrobamiento,* or rapture. But I call it *abobamiento,* foolishness" (pp. 92-93).

[10] For some papal documents on the Rosary, see *Papal Teachings: The Holy Rosary,* selected and arranged by the Benedictine Monks of

Also, the Rosary is a safe way to God. It prevents one from falling into the errors of the Quietists. The faith and humility that comes with the childlike simplicity of this prayer are built-in defenses against the devil's traps.

Saint John of the Cross observes that there are many aspirants who reach the gate of perfection, but only few actually enter it. I think that more proficients will *actually enter* the age of the perfect if they pray the Rosary daily. This is because Mary herself is the "gate of heaven," as we say in the Litany. They who pray the Rosary daily will pass through the Night of the Spirit successfully. For it is the Blessed Mother Herself who will hold them by the hand as their fingers run through the beads of their dark yet loving prayers. Even for those who are in the active life, the Rosary is a source of strength and heavenly lights. While praying, and after each Rosary, they understand better the God that they love. Their devotion to Mary breaks the last thin thread that prevents them from flying to the summit of perfection.

Therefore, let us not underestimate the power of Mary's intercession. By propagating the Rosary, Saint Dominic healed many souls, converted many sinners, and vanquished the heresy that once

Solesmes, tr. by Rev. Paul J. Oligny, OFM (Boston, MA: The Daughters of Saint Paul, 1980).

threatened all of Christendom. History is full of examples of good people who became devout, and pious souls who became saints, through their unfailing devotion to Mary. Through the recitation of the holy Rosary battles were won and entire nations saved.[11] Saint Louis Marie de Montfort affirmed that the Holy Rosary is so powerful that it can rescue even a soul that has already been sold to the devil.[12] This is not surprising. For God has decided to fight the Enemy through Mary, a fact that has been revealed since the beginning of humankind: "I will put enmity between you and the woman, and your seed and her seed: she shall crush your head, and you shall lie in wait for her heel" (Gn 3:15).[13]

---

[11] I have in mind, for example, the Battle of Lepanto and the La Naval de Manila, both of which were won through the intercession of the Blessed Virgin Mary.

[12] Saint Louis Marie de Montfort, *op. cit.*, Dedication to Sinners, p. 12.

[13] This text is from the Douay version of the Bible, which is a literal English rendering of Saint Jerome's Latin Vulgate. I am aware that the new Catholic Bibles today translate this passage as "*He* will strike at your head and you shall lie in wait for *his* heel," the pronoun "He" referring messianically to Jesus (the "seed" or "offspring") since the antecedent for "he" and "his" is the collective noun, "offspring" rather than to Mary (the "woman"). I do not wish to join the debate regarding this. Various copies of the Hebrew text are actually ambiguous, as Saint Bellarmine observes. If we apply the Hebrew literary law of parallelism, however, then the context would seem to suggest the pronoun to refer to the woman rather than to her seed. On this basis, a genuinely possible translation of the pronoun, as I have indicated, is "She" rather than "He."

This book was designed and published by St. Pauls/Alba House, the publishing arm of the Society of St. Paul, an international religious congregation of priests and brothers dedicated to serving the Church through the communications media. For information regarding this and associated ministries of the Pauline Family of Congregations, write to the Vocation Director, Society of St. Paul, 7050 Pinehurst, Dearborn, Michigan 48126 or check our internet site, www.albahouse.org